"*Cultivating Mentors* illustrates m[...] relational mentoring in an incre[...] on faculty flourishing and studen[...] [...]ults of rapidly changing academic and professional environments, this timely volume directs educators to practical tools for cultivating faith and vocational discernment in tandem with fostering a powerful sense of faith-based community on their university campuses."
Karen A. Lee, provost and professor of English at Wheaton College

"This book is aimed especially at leaders of Christian higher education who, in an age of digitization and diversity, are recruiting the next generation of teacher-scholars for their schools. The contributors ground their assessment in a theology of vocation, they are alert to the changing culture of contemporary young adults, and they offer hard-won wisdom concerning the institutional dynamics of colleges and universities. Careful attention to theory seasoned by numerous specific examples make for unusually compelling reading."
Mark A. Noll, Francis A. McAnaney Professor of History Emeritus, University of Notre Dame

"The editors of *Cultivating Mentors* have enlisted an outstanding group of experienced Christian educators who highlight the challenges of the younger generation of Christians, in particular Millennials and Gen Z, as revealed in thousands of interviews conducted by the Barna Group. The authors provide specific proposals to administrators for providing helpful mentoring for junior faculty at Christian colleges."
Edwin M. Yamauchi, professor of history emeritus, Miami University

"The context for mentoring has changed enormously in recent years, and the roles of mentor and mentee now frequently oscillate. *Cultivating Mentors* explores this new terrain where generational differences and cultural diversities are taken seriously and where personal flourishing receives intensified attention. With insights from a multitude of organizational and generational perspectives, this volume will encourage fresh thinking across the full spectrum of institutional roles in Christian higher education."
Douglas Jacobsen and **Rhonda Hustedt Jacobsen,** authors of *Scholarship and Christian Faith*

"The lasting impact and endurance of our Christian universities relies squarely on the strength and vitality of each generation of leaders—from student to professor to president—to sustain the mission through challenging times. Who among us in academia can imagine succeeding without forerunners who mentor us by making 'a way in the wilderness'? *Cultivating Mentors* is a volume that places a call on each of us to cultivate collegial relationships at every age and stage to produce flourishing careers for flourishing institutions. With an impressive cadre of contributors that spans various roles within higher education, this book offers valuable insight and encouragement for all on the journey."
Steven D. Mason, president and professor of Old Testament studies at LeTourneau University

"Scripture is replete with commands of cherishing ancient wisdom, living under truth, and teaching it to the next generations. Mentoring colleagues and students in higher education is one way to obey these commands in our vocation. The voices in this volume helps us be faithful in the good work of mentoring, from generation to generation. May the words herein provide instruction and inspiration to be faithful stewards of such a trust."

Edee Schulze, vice president for student life at Westmont College

"This outstanding book brings together desperately needed fresh thinking on mentorship from scholars who are real-life beneficiaries and practitioners of mentoring. These essays offer a kaleidoscopic look at the beauty of theologically informed mentorship and show us why it is so necessary. We can all be thankful that such a thoughtful guidebook is now available at this kairos moment in Christian higher education."

Todd L. Lake, vice president for spiritual development at Belmont University

"Good mentorship is one of the most powerful and sacred relationships we can offer to the future generation of leaders. This book is an invaluable resource for helping us think about how to establish and sustain these relationships."

Nancy Brickhouse, provost and professor of education at Baylor University

CULTIVATING
MENTORS

CULTIVATING
MENTORS

SHARING WISDOM IN
CHRISTIAN HIGHER EDUCATION

EDITED BY

Todd C. Ream, Jerry Pattengale,
and Christopher J. Devers

FOREWORD BY Mark R. Schwehn

ivp
Academic
An imprint of InterVarsity Press
Downers Grove, Illinois

InterVarsity Press
P.O. Box 1400 | Downers Grove, IL 60515-1426
ivpress.com | email@ivpress.com

©2022 by Todd C. Ream, Jerry A. Pattengale, and Christopher J. Devers

All rights reserved. No part of this book may be reproduced in any form without written permission from InterVarsity Press.

InterVarsity Press® is the publishing division of InterVarsity Christian Fellowship/USA®. For more information, visit intervarsity.org.

Scripture quotations, unless otherwise noted, are from the New Revised Standard Version Bible, copyright © 1989 National Council of the Churches of Christ in the United States of America. Used by permission. All rights reserved worldwide.

While any stories in this book are true, some names and identifying information may have been changed to protect the privacy of individuals.

The publisher cannot verify the accuracy or functionality of website URLs used in this book beyond the date of publication.

Cover design and image composite: David Fassett
Interior design: Jeanna Wiggins

ISBN 978-1-5140-0253-7 (casebound) | ISBN 978-1-5140-0252-0 (paperback) | ISBN 978-1-5140-0254-4 (digital)

Printed in the United States of America ♾

Library of Congress Cataloging-in-Publication Data
A catalog record for this book is available from the Library of Congress.

29 28 27 26 25 24 23 22 | 8 7 6 5 4 3 2 1

TO DAVID W. WRIGHT

With gratitude

for your years of service

as an educator, leader,

and mentor

CONTENTS

FOREWORD

MARK R. SCHWEHN

When Caroline Simon and her several colleagues finished their little book *Mentoring for Mission: Nurturing New Faculty at Church-Related Colleges* in 2003, they could not have known that they were unleashing what would become, over the course of the next twenty years, a veritable herd of books about mentoring in many fields of human endeavor. Simon, then a professor of philosophy at Hope College and later provost at Whitworth University, had a captive audience for the book she introduced and edited. It was developed as a resource for a growing network of church-related colleges and universities across the country: the Lilly Fellows Program's (LFP) National Network of Church-Related Colleges and Universities. Many of the schools in that network had applied for mini-grants to support the development of mentoring programs for new faculty, and as these programs mushroomed in number and variety, the LFP encouraged Simon and others to write the book as a resource for faculty who wanted to serve as mentors to their junior colleagues. The book was for many years used at church-related schools both inside and outside of the LFP.

The present book, *Cultivating Mentors: Sharing Wisdom in Christian Higher Education*, responds exceptionally well to the momentous changes that have overtaken the church-related academy and all of American culture over the years since 2003. Most young men and women in the labor force today are either Millennials (b. 1980–1994 and representing 50 percent of the workforce in the US today) or Generation Zers (b. 1995–2015). Though glib characterizations of generational cohorts are problematic, there can be no doubt that people entering the work force today, unlike most of those who serve as their mentors, take the internet for granted, are fully at home within the world of social media, often believe that the idea of a work "place" is antiquated, and sometimes prefer Google to a senior colleague as a mentor. The convulsive effects of information technology and, more recently, Covid-19 on social and geographical mobility, personal identity, the workplace economy, and vocational choice are not as yet fully understood. By comparison to the young people who were coming of age in 2003, today's young people are less theologically literate and less likely to seek spiritual fulfillment in established churches. And these are just a few of the ways in which the world of today differs profoundly from the world that Simon and her colleagues faced a mere twenty years ago.

The editors and contributors of the present volume develop many strategies to address the challenge of mentoring today's young faculty members at church-related colleges. Most obviously, the book enlarges perspectives beyond faculty. The practical wisdom about mentoring offered here comes from faculty, administrators, leadership-training professionals, and specialists who have studied one or another of the major changes itemized above. This multiperspectival approach yields several essays that draw on the wisdom of the Christian tradition in order to engage the challenges of mentoring in today's turbulent environment.

All of the authors connect the project of mentoring within the Christian academy to the Christian idea of the academic vocation. Though the theological vocabulary of vocation is often unfamiliar to young people today, the authors repeatedly point out that the idea of vocation addresses precisely those concerns foremost on the minds and hearts of contemporaries —questions of meaning, purpose, significance, identity, and integrity. Moreover, the Christian emphases on divine summoning and communal discernment enrich and enlarge such widespread preoccupations with spiritual depth and devotional practices.

Any encounter between a tradition of thought and practice on the one hand and a host of new ideas and personalities on the other yields fresh insights and practical innovations. The present book offers a feast of these. For example, given the growing differences between most mentors and their mentees, the project of mentoring becomes much more dialogical.

Mentees can instruct mentors about information technology at the same time that mentors can instruct mentees about the Christian idea of vocation. And institutions need to change in order to accommodate the needs of mentees as much as mentees need to adjust and broaden their understandings as they absorb the ethos, the mythos, and the logos of their new communities. Mentoring was never a one-way street, since within the Christian academy it was always a collegially spiritual enterprise. But as the contributors to this book show repeatedly, it must be even more collaborative and communal today.

Perhaps the major change to have overtaken the church-related academy over the last generation is captured by the two watchwords *diversity* and *inclusion*. When diversity designates, as it should, not only a variety of racial and ethnic groups but also a variety of faiths, socioeconomic classes, cultural backgrounds, and sexual orientations, it holds out the prospect of enlivening and enriching communities of inquiry of all kinds. This great cultural opportunity has been realized far beyond the church-related academy in business, industry, the fine arts, and even legal theory and practice. At the same time, however, the tasks of keeping particular traditions alive and transmitting them across generations have become more and more challenging. Living traditions are, at their best, dynamic and responsive, and diverse groups within the academy are, at their best, parts of a larger community quest for the truth of matters. Tradition keeps diversity from becoming mere chaotic fragmentation, even as diversity keeps tradition from becoming a snug and insular ossification. Christians seek engaged, constructive, loving, fallibilistic pluralism, not pointless and destructive strife.

These abstract ideals are easy to state but increasingly difficult to realize within our sometimes violently polarized country. So one needs to specify mechanisms by which and through which tradition and diversity can be drawn together into productive tension or deeper harmonies. As this book makes clear, mentoring is quite possibly the best practice for achieving these delicate balances. Only in finely attuned, intentional conversations extended over time can Christian academic communities reap the continued blessings arising from a diversity of gifts in the one Spirit, from a variety of backgrounds and beliefs directed to a common inquiry. One might even argue that mentoring is not a means or mechanism for creating a healthy Christian academic community; rather, it is the very constitution of that community in practice.

We all owe the many contributors to this volume our thanks for strengthening and informing our faith in that promise.

ACKNOWLEDGMENTS

One irony of the coronavirus pandemic was its ability to foster gratitude for people who sacrificed so much during those difficult years. While most scholars did not bear the burdens physicians, nurses, and K-12 teachers and administrators did during that season, life was not easy. We learned flexibility and relied on the goodwill of others to do the same. Despite the acrimony that engulfed the American public square, we were blessed to work with a host of people on this project who, despite the challenges, made the process a joy.

First, that list of people includes the contributors who lent their wisdom to this volume. When exploring a practice such as mentoring, we could not have asked for a group more distinguished than one that includes David Kinnaman, Tim Clydesdale, Margaret Diddams, Edgardo Colón-Emeric, Rebecca C. Hong, Tim Elmore, and Beck A. Taylor. During this season, several of them accepted new positions, made cross-country moves, and, as with so many, experienced loss. Despite "pivots" (an overused word we now loathe) made, they persevered and made exceptional contributions from which we are optimistic you will benefit greatly. Perhaps most important, they were a joy to work with.

Second, we are blessed to count Jon Boyd and his colleagues at Inter-Varsity Press as valued colleagues and friends. Over the course of our respective careers, we have worked with an array of university presses and trade publishers. None of them come close to the quality of efforts Jon and his colleagues make on behalf of their authors. When the pandemic prompted the postponement of the September 2021 "Mentoring Matters" symposium to September 2022, Jon proposed we go ahead with the production of this volume and release it when the symposium was finally able

to commence. While we were essentially done with our work, we knew the pressures such a timeline would put on Jon and his colleagues. As always, their commitment to their authors proved unquestioned and a model for their profession.

Third, we are honored that Mark R. Schwehn agreed to offer the foreword for this volume. Perhaps no one has thought more deeply about the academic vocation and the practice of mentoring than Mark. His *Exiles from Eden* is a classic reflection on the calling we all share. The countless lives he touched as a mentor, however, are the greatest measure of the virtues that define him. Having his words open this volume is an honor.

Fourth, the Lilly Fellows Program (an effort Mark played a key role in launching) became a valued partner in this project. Through their generosity, we were able to gather teams of leaders from Indiana's Catholic and evangelical colleges and universities for the symposium at a time when the pandemic placed budgets in states of great uncertainty. As the leaders of the Lilly Fellows Program, Joe Creech and Jenna Van Sickle are to be credited for the patience and encouragement they shared with us as we navigated the pandemic. As with the others mentioned here, we are grateful to now call them friends and colleagues.

Fifth, freelance editor extraordinaire Evelyn Bence deserves considerable credit for keeping us out of the weeds in more ways than we can count. Few can focus on both the macro and micro-level details as well as Evelyn. Her abilities to fact-check, think through the flow of argumentation (or lack thereof), and polish style make her a critical partner in this project for whom we are truly grateful.

Finally, Indiana Wesleyan University's former president David W. Wright and former provost Stacy Hammons entrusted us with the responsibility of launching the Lumen Research Institute about eight years ago. In partnership with friends at Excelsia College in Macquarie Park, New South Wales, Lumen emerged as "a global collective of Christian scholars who pursue questions of social concern through collaborative and interdisciplinary research efforts." As we finish this third project, we are launching our fourth, "Habits of Hope." We are optimistic these projects are a worthy response to the confidence David and Stacy invested in us.

When the time comes, we are also hopeful these projects laid the foundation for a scholarly institute worthy of passing along to colleagues we mentor.

In December 2021, David announced his intention to retire as Indiana Wesleyan University's president at the conclusion of the 2021–2022 academic year. As we noted, Lumen's existence is largely the result of his vision for Indiana Wesleyan University and the future of Christian higher education. With great peace, he weathered the pandemic and rightfully deserves the opportunity now to focus on other pursuits (rumor has it that he is building his own airplane). After some well-deserved rest, we look forward to welcoming him as Lumen's Senior Fellow for Global Partnerships. With gratitude for his years of service as an educator, leader, and mentor, we dedicate this volume to David.

Todd C. Ream

Jerry Pattengale

Christopher J. Devers

INTRODUCTION

A Season of Peril?

TODD C. REAM, JERRY PATTENGALE,
AND CHRISTOPHER J. DEVERS

Until she began her second year of teaching, Marvilla believed the decisions she made concerning her vocation as a Christian scholar and as a person were not only professionally prudent but honoring of her relationship with God. Growing up in a Pentecostal family and church in South Texas, Marvilla was the first in her family and one of the first in her church to go to college. Knowing God had given her considerable intellectual abilities, Marvilla's parents and fellow church members were thrilled when she chose to attend a Christian college, even if it meant she traveled over one thousand miles away from home.

Marvilla flourished while in college as both curricular and cocurricular educators recognized her considerable abilities. As a political science major and Spanish minor, she was asked by professors to work with them on various projects. This gave her the opportunity to give several conference papers and publish a couple of articles, including her senior thesis. Her residence director encouraged her to run for various student government positions, which culminated in her service as student body president her senior year.

Now thirteen hundred miles away from home, Marvilla experienced continued support while in graduate school, where she earned several fellowships, traveled widely in Central and South America to conduct research, and coauthored what became an award-winning book with her adviser. Those efforts led Marvilla to have the luxury of choosing between several tenure-track positions in political science. Eighteen hundred miles from her family and church in South Texas, Marvilla proudly accepted an offer from a Christian college.

The first year of teaching proved demanding, but Marvilla weathered the transition, believing she was making a positive impact on the students she served. Her course evaluations were high, and she established a research group with several second- and third-year students, developed a study abroad partnership, and, although she admittedly knew little about softball, became the faculty adviser for the college's intercollegiate team.

Despite spending ample time on campus, Marvilla eventually noticed relationships with her colleagues remained somewhat distant. Most of them demonstrated little interest in her research and even less interest in her life as a young, single Latina. Closest to her own age was a colleague who was nine years older than Marvilla. All of her colleagues were also White, married, and spent little to no time on research. When a prominent university press published her dissertation as a book, none of her colleagues took notice. When that same publisher offered her a contract for a second book, some of her colleagues began exhibiting passive-aggressive forms of hostility. Despite evidence to the contrary offered by Marvilla's teaching evaluations, questions began circulating as to whether Marvilla's commitment to research meant she was not committed to teaching.

Seeking to make sense of the mounting vocational and personal disorientation she was feeling, Marvilla decided to seek a mentor's wisdom. When looking for a mentor, however, she could not find someone who shared her passions for teaching, research, and service. Compounding the challenge, she could not find someone who shared in her life story as a young, single Latina. Marvilla's vocational disorientation would only grow with each passive-aggressive comment. Lacking a mentor's insights, Marvilla failed to determine that the reason for those comments was mounting professional jealousy. As she waded into her second year of teaching, Marvilla began to wonder if she had made a mistake. She wondered if not only her identity as a Christian scholar but also her value as a person created in God's image was in peril.

MENTORING, GENERATIONAL TRANSITION, AND THE ACADEMIC VOCATION

Framed by insights from the Christian theological tradition, this volume explores ideas about and approaches to the practice of mentoring, asking what that tradition has to offer scholars such as Marvilla. In particular, the volume responds to the needs of younger generations (e.g., Millennials and Gen Z) as they enter the academic workforce. It considers how traditional Christian ideas around academic vocation and theologically informed practices of mentoring can be used to support those educators.

As a whole, this distinguished group of contributors explores the practice of mentoring from the past, drawing on traditional, theological understandings of the mentee-mentor relationship to consider what goals should define mentoring relationships in the future and what practices make the cultivation of those relationships possible. This volume thereby offers important theoretical insights and practical recommendations for scholars, faculty members, student affairs professionals, and policy makers.

In order to do so, this volume builds on three commonly accepted notions: (1) younger generations present specific and previously unseen needs and characteristics as they enter higher education; (2) these individuals may well benefit from mentorship, which, as yet, remains fairly ill-defined in relation to concrete applications; and (3) the Christian tradition embraces ideas of mentorship within the academic vocation. As such, the volume explores traditionally theological approaches to the practice of mentoring to consider how far they might be applied effectively to support young people in Christian, as well as other secular institutions in higher education.

To those ends, this volume includes explorations of the characteristics and needs of younger generations including Millennials (born between 1980 and 1994) and Gen Z (born between 1995 and 2015). Qualities represented by members of these generations are often perceived as sources of friction in the workplace. For example, in the February 19, 2020, edition of the *New York Times*, Jasmine Hughes offered "Need to Keep Gen Z Workers Happy? Hire a 'Generational Consultant.'"

Many sociologists point to a heightened need to raise such questions with members of these younger generations. For example, David Kinnaman, president of the Barna Group and contributor to this volume, noted in relation to his study of Millennials and the church titled *You Lost Me*, that "the next generation's prodigious use of technology, entertainment, and media" is historically significant.[1] In particular, such forms and rates of usage disconnect them from members of previous generations and, in turn, influence how well members of younger generations inherit those roles. Kinnaman suggests mentoring practices focused on the cultivation of vocational awareness and wisdom as ways to address that challenge.

Regardless of what one thinks of Millennials and members of Gen Z, they are gradually taking on roles and entering the workforce in positions formerly held by members of the Baby Boomer generation. The Millennial generation alone, for example, now makes up approximately half of the workforce in the United States. Resisting the changes represented by Millennials and members of Gen Z is not only pragmatically misguided, but also precludes an appreciation of positive qualities that Millennials and members of Gen Z may be introducing to the workforce. For example, in the September 17, 2019, issue of the *New York Times*, Claire Cain Miller and Sanam Yar proposed, "Could they [Millennials], instead, be among the first to understand the proper role of work in life—and end up remaking work for everyone else?"[2]

This volume pays particular attention to the potential role of these generations in the academic workforce. A central argument of the volume is that instead of demeaning or resisting the changes in expectations members of younger generations represent, colleges and universities would be well served by engaging these changes. As Miller and Yar propose, a greater awareness of the relationship shared by work and life can be utilized as a means of helping colleges and universities fulfill their missions at higher levels than members of previous generations had envisioned. A

---

[1]David Kinnaman, *You Lost Me: Why Young Christians Are Leaving Church . . . and Rethinking Faith* (Grand Rapids, MI: Baker Books, 2011), 41.
[2]Claire Cain Miller and Sanam Yar, "Young People Are Going to Save Us All from Office Life," *New York Times*, September 17, 2019, www.nytimes.com/2019/09/17/style/generation-z-millennials -work-life-balance.html.

second core argument is that mentorship is critical to cultivating what the younger generation can offer as educators.

In support of this assertion, this volume explores ways of supporting members of these generations by developing theologically informed and effective approaches to the practice of mentoring. College admissions materials, for example, are littered with images of faculty providing students with advice over coffee and working side by side on research. New colleagues are often recruited with the promise of access to wisdom offered by accomplished colleagues. Regardless, definitions of mentoring, as well as concrete organizational commitments to good mentoring, are nearly non-existent.

Perhaps for the very reason that the value of mentoring is perceived to be self-evident, scholars, regardless of discipline, pay little attention to debating the goals of mentoring, what practices allow for the achievement of those goals, and what challenges may emerge when those goals are not rightfully defined and honored. For example, the results of a poll conducted by Gallup and released on January 24, 2019, demonstrated the link between student well-being and support from faculty. However, the summary of the results of that poll suggested, "supportive relationships with professors and mentors are significantly more common in certain fields of study—including arts and humanities—than others."[3] One challenge lurking within the details is that the goal of mentoring went undefined and, as a result, the practices allowing that goal to be achieved went unnamed.

Ubiquitous perceptions of the value of mentoring are arguably even more pervasive on evangelical university campuses than on other campuses. The Christian commitment to hospitality, naming only one such commitment, fosters environments where the benefits of practices such as mentoring are assumed. The goals and attendant mentoring practices on those campuses, however, are subject to little to no critical reflection. The unquestioned nature of those assumptions raises the possibility that some mentoring practices may even be more harmful than beneficial.

[3]Steve Crabtree, "Student Support from Faculty, Mentors Varies by Major," Gallup, January 24, 2019, https://news.gallup.com/poll/246017/student-support-faculty-mentors-varies-major.aspx.

This volume thus argues the Christian theological tradition offers a wealth of knowledge and experience in relation to mentorship. Such critical reflection may usefully inform new and effective approaches to support Millennials and members of Gen Z through effective mentor-mentee relationships. As a result, exploring those practices in this sector of higher education may yield best practices that may prove applicable to higher education more broadly. To that end, this volume:

1. considers the characteristics of younger generations in the context of mentoring,
2. explores what the Christian tradition offers in terms of mentorship and academic vocation, and
3. demonstrates how these ideas might inform mentorship of members of younger generations in broader scholarly contexts.

MENTORING, GENERATIONAL TRANSITION, AND THE ACADEMIC VOCATION

While many books exist concerning members of younger generations and mentoring, and a few even exist concerning the academic vocation, no book considers the three of them and the relationship they share. This book does so, and does so in a way, again, that frames that relationship by drawing on the riches of the Christian theological tradition. What follows then is an overview of key resources utilized in the development of the argument defining this book, many of which were generated by contributors to this book.

First, many of the books related to members of younger generations amount to manuals for members of other generations seeking to manage them—for example, please see Chris Tuff's *The Millennial Whisperer* (Morgan James, 2019) and Bruce Tulgan's *Not Everyone Gets a Trophy* (Jossey-Bass, 2016). In terms of members of younger generations and insights about their spiritual lives, the work done by Tim Clydesdale (as evidenced by his recent *The Twentysomething Soul: Understanding the Religious and Secular Lives of American Young Adults*, Oxford University Press, 2019) proved to be beneficial to defining the commitments shaping this project. Fortunately, he is also a contributor to this volume.

In addition, David Kinnaman has focused his attention for years on the spiritual lives of younger generations, publishing works such as *Faith for Exiles: 5 Ways for a New Generation to Follow Jesus in Digital Babylon* (Baker Books, 2019), *Good Faith: Being a Christian When Society Thinks You're Irrelevant and Extreme* (Baker Books, 2016), *You Lost Me: Why Young Christians Are Leaving Church . . . and Rethinking Faith* (Baker Books, 2011), and *unChristian: What a New Generation Really Thinks about Christianity . . . and Why It Matters* (Baker Books, 2007).

For almost twenty years, Christian Smith has traced the spiritual lives of members of younger generations as they passed from being teenagers to emerging adults. While his *Soul Searching: The Religious and Spiritual Lives of American Teenagers* (Oxford University Press, 2005) proved helpful, his *Souls in Transition: The Religious and Spiritual Lives of Emerging Adults* (Oxford University Press, 2009), and *Lost in Transition: The Dark Side of Emerging Adulthood* (Oxford University Press, 2011) proved beneficial to defining the commitments shaping this project.

As evident in the chapters that follow, how generations are defined and, in particular, the value those definitions offer is still a matter for debate. Some scholars place considerable value on the characteristics represented by various generations. Others are less confident. One summary of some of those debates and differences is found in Bobby Duffy's *The Generation Myth: Why When You're Born Matters Less than You Think* (Basic Books, 2021).

Regardless of one's views of such debates, oversimplifications can result in situations that fail to develop practices supporting members of these generations while also acknowledging their changed perceptions, strengths, and existence in a much-changed world. Such oversimplifications, and the challenges that follow, are not always limited to being projected on members of younger generations. Helen Andrews's *Boomers: The Men and Women Who Promised Freedom and Delivered Disaster* (Sentinel, 2021) is a prime example of the challenges that form of generational oversimplification, albeit in the reverse order often exercised, can offer.

While a seemingly endless number of volumes exist concerning mentoring, very few are based on theological reflection or empirical assessment.

As previously indicated, many titles present mentoring as an unquestioned good and then move quickly to offering tips or strategies. Resources that begin to point beyond those books, however, are Tammy D. Allen and Lillian T. Eby's (eds.) *Blackwell Handbook of Mentoring: A Multiple Perspectives Approach* (Wiley-Blackwell, 2010) and Jean E. Rhodes's *Older and Wiser: New Ideas for Youth Mentoring in the 21st Century* (Harvard University Press, 2020).

When one looks for works on the mentoring of collegiate educators, only a handful emerges, including David Kiel's *Developing Faculty Mentoring Programs: A Comprehensive Handbook* (Academic Impressions, 2019); Susan L. Phillips and Milton D. Cox's *Faculty Mentoring: A Practical Manual for Mentors, Mentees, Administrators, and Faculty Developers* (Stylus, 2015); Peter Felton, H. Dirksen L. Bauman, Aaron Kheriaty, and Edward Taylor's (eds.) *Transformative Conversations: A Guide to Mentoring Communities Among Colleagues in Higher Education* (Jossey-Bass, 2013); Dwayne Mack, Elwood D. Watson, and Michelle Madsen Camacho's (eds.) *Mentoring Faculty of Color: Essays on Professional Development and Advancement in Colleges and Universities* (McFarland & Company, 2012); and Carole J. Bland, Anne L. Taylor, S. Lynn Shollen, Anne Marie Weber-Main, and Patricia A. Mulcahy's *Faculty Success Through Mentoring: A Guide for Mentors, Mentees, and Leaders* (Rowman & Littlefield, 2009).

While only one chapter in Michael G. Strawser's (ed.) *Leading Millennial Faculty: Navigating the New Professoriate* (Lexington, 2019) focuses directly on mentoring, that chapter, as well as several other related chapters, also proved beneficial to defining the commitments shaping this project. Caroline J. Simon's edited volume *Mentoring for Mission: Nurturing New Faculty at Church-Related Colleges* (Eerdmans, 2003) provided optimism that a theology of mentoring was applicable to cultivating an appreciation for the Christian academic vocation.

The literature base that is probably the most lacking but is just as foundational to this project is that which explores the academic vocation. Countless descriptive studies focus on collegiate educators but only a few focus on the theological contours that define what it means to be called to such a profession. The most notable work and the one that greatly shaped this project is Mark R. Schwehn's *Exiles from Eden: Religion and the Academic Vocation* (Oxford University Press, 1999). A more recent volume that demonstrates considerable promise for understanding the academic vocation is Shaun C. Henson and Michael J. Lakey's *Academic Vocation in the Church and Academy Today: 'And with All of Your Mind'* (Routledge, 2016).

VOLUME OVERVIEW

In order to grapple with how the practice of mentoring can deepen an appreciation for the academic vocation during seasons of generational transition, this volume includes contributions from distinguished scholars who graciously offer their scholarly insights and programmatic advice.

Chapter one, "The Need to Rediscover: Mentoring as a Crucial Formation Practice," David Kinnaman: A critical component to understanding members of younger generations is coming to terms with how they are theologically oriented. As some scholars note, "Nones" have no formal religious commitments. For the majority, however, their comparatively diverse theological convictions are not only critical to how they understand themselves, but also to how they orient their lives as a whole. In contrast, Baby Boomers were often viewed as having more homogeneous theological convictions, but many also viewed those commitments as best defining their private lives. For younger individuals with or without theological commitments, little to no disjunction between public and private exists. Mentorship enables individuals to explore how faith and learning relate to one another and indicates how that relationship can serve educators as they progress in their careers.

Chapter two, "Leading Integrated Lives: Navigating Personal and Professional Commitments Through Mentorship," Tim Clydesdale: The forces that led to the rise of the phase in life now known as emerging adulthood (cost of living, length of time in school, delayed time to marriage and childbearing, etc.) contributed to the appreciation members of younger generations now have for the practice of mentoring. The mentoring they appreciate is not simply focused on what jobs they choose, but processing what theological commitments or values led them to pursue such professional roles. However, mentoring need not conclude once individuals decide to serve as collegiate educators and begin careers. Mentorship theologically resources educators striving to understand the relationship between their personal and professional lives and then how to navigate that relationship if it changes over the course of their lives.

Chapter three, "Call and Response: Mentoring for Organizational Fit and Flourishing," Margaret Diddams: While members of younger generations are more suspicious of organizations or institutions than members of previous generations, they often value community at a higher level. If prepared well, the values they hold have the potential to re-shape institutions, in general, and colleges and universities, in particular, in ways that will allow those institutions to fulfill their missions in ways previous generations were theologically not capable of envisioning. In the meantime, the transition in how members of different generations understand the institutions they inhabit may come with challenges. Collegiate educators need to be prepared to face those challenges, understand why they are occurring, and, whenever possible, theologically view them as opportunities for growth. Mentorship theologically resources young educators coming to terms with how they think about organizations, as well as what assumptions they employ when thinking about what it means to be individuals who exist in larger organizational and institutional contexts.

Chapter four, "Diversity and Community: Mentoring Toward a New *We*," Edgardo Colón-Emeric: One dynamic reshaping almost all institutions is growing ethnic diversity. Members of younger generations are not only more ethnically diverse than members of previous generations, but they also tend to place a greater value on ethnic diversity. While commendable, calls for diversity provoke both opposition as well as support in a culture presently defined by social and political polarization. In order to fulfill a theologically rooted understanding of diversity, what then do collegiate educators need to do to create environments that not only tolerate difference, but welcome and appreciate it? Answers to that question will prove critical to ways institutions will not only change but hopefully also evolve. Building on this exploration, mentorship aids individuals in processing what theological commitments they possess concerning ethnic diversity as well as how those commitments come together within organizational and institutional contexts.

Chapter five, "Boomers and Zoomers: Mentoring Toward Human-Centeredness in Our Work," Rebecca C. Hong: Members of younger generations are the first to live as digital natives or individuals for whom cell phones and social media platforms existed for the majority of their lives. Their practices and habits of communication are different from members of previous generations, as well as their expectations concerning where, when, and how they work. On one level, they do not view work as something done at a particular place, at a particular time, and in a particular way. On another level, they desire greater flexibility in terms of where, when, and how work is completed. Exacerbated by the coronavirus pandemic, such shifts have ramifications not only for the completion of work but also for the fabric of institutions that work is intended to advance. Educators populating different generations will need to understand those changes and at least initially view them as theologically informed opportunities for work to be completed at higher levels even if that work is being done at different times, in different places, and perhaps even in different ways. Mentorship draws on theological ideas concerning to what end we work and, in turn, informs where, when, and how we work.

Chapter six, "Intentional Influence: Relevant Practices and Habits We Must Cultivate in Today's Emerging Generation," Tim Elmore: Ultimately, organizations are collections of cultural expectations shaped by virtue of the participation of community members in common practices that eventually come to fruition in habits. Regardless of what commonalities they share, part of what makes universities different is the habits that respectively define them. Despite their commonalities, no two university communities are ever defined by the exact same habits. However, how often do community members take time to think theologically about the expectations that define their institutions, along with the practices and habits that make those expectations possible? Perhaps one point in time when those expectations become evident is when members of a subsequent generation begin accepting positions within the community. Instead of generational transition being a time when friction surfaces over those expectations, what would it mean for educators to participate in collaborative and on-going processes that would allow them to think theologically about those expectations? In response to this question, colleges and universities might adopt theologically informed mentorship. Doing so would encourage collaborative reflection between younger and older educators as they consider the historical expectations that define their institutions, and then perhaps inform how those expectations are refined, rejected, and/or reimagined.

Chapter seven, "Who Will Lead Us: A Lifecycle Approach to Academic Mentorship," Beck A. Taylor: At the present time, Millennials and members of Gen Z are growing in number in ranks such as residence directors, academic advisers, assistant coaches, and assistant professors. In the near future, those same colleagues will begin populating positions such as directors of residence life, head coaches, department chairs, and full professors. Eventually, they will serve as chief academic affairs officers, chief student affairs officers, and presidents. Instead of simply mentoring members of those generations to serve well in those entry-level roles as educators, what would it mean to mentor them to one day serve well when they are senior administrators? What theological lessons, then, prepare them to lead well now *and* in the future? A process of addressing those questions does not begin when individuals assume senior-level positions but years earlier, shortly after they arrive on campus and take entry-level ones. Mentorship theologically resources younger educators to engage with the prospect of leadership, the qualities leadership requires, and the question of how they can nurture and strengthen those qualities within themselves and others.

Conclusion, "A Season of Promise," Stacy Hammons: Drawing from the material proposed in the introduction and the seven chapters that followed it, the conclusion focuses on a summation of what was offered and then translates those details into propositions educators will need to consider. Doing so then allows the future to be viewed as one defined by the promise it offers. As members of younger generations continue to take their place as collegiate educators and, in time, as athletic directors, chief academic affairs officers, chief student affairs officers, and presidents, universities may be poised to fulfill their missions at levels higher than members of previous generations envisioned. Mentorship theologically resources individuals attempting to align the potential of those expectations at the highest possible levels.

FROM PERIL TO PROMISE

Although she did not want to leave the college where she began her teaching career, Marvilla eventually came to believe she had no other choice. As successes with her students and in her field mounted, so did the passive aggressive comments from her colleagues. No longer able to mask her professional jealousy, one of Marvilla's colleagues, her department chair, began lashing out at her. Those experiences became so unfortunate that Marvilla started insisting they only meet in public spaces such as the coffee counter in the student center. Marvilla eventually accepted an offer from another college due to mounting fears that even her promotion to associate professor was in question.

Moving is never easy. In Marvilla's case, however, the sacrifice proved worthwhile. Marvilla's new colleagues honored her work. Team-taught courses, coauthored papers and books, co-led study abroad programs, and departmental coffee hours defined the culture Marvilla came to share with her new colleagues. When the softball team needed a new faculty adviser, Marvilla was also eager to serve. Just as important in Marvilla's success was a mentor who sought her out shortly after her arrival.

That mentor, a prominent faculty member in economics, helped Marvilla navigate the institutional politics, set a long-term research agenda, find a church, and connect with a leadership succession program for young women. Although now two thousand miles away from her home in South Texas, Marvilla found a community that valued her promise as a Christian scholar and as a person created in God's image.

1

THE NEED TO REDISCOVER

Mentoring as a Crucial Formation Process

DAVID KINNAMAN

Since 1995, I have had the privilege of conducting social research focused primarily on the intersection of cultural trends and societal changes and the faith beliefs and practices of people in the United States and across the globe. It is the mission of Barna, the company I lead, to help Christians, pastors, church and parachurch ministry leaders, and leaders of Christian colleges and universities "understand the times and know what to do." Like the biblical tribe of Issachar, Barna exists to make sense of what's happening in the world: to provide data-informed insights so that leaders can adapt and develop to meet the needs of people living in this ever-changing world.

For the past fifteen years, our team has worked hard to understand global youth and the young adult culture of Millennials (born between 1984 and 1998) and Gen Z (born between 1999 and 2015). I'm especially interested in their spiritual formation—how we can disciple young people in the Christian faith.

In this chapter, I'll address the process of Christian formation for the next generation—how we can make a real difference in the lives of young people based on findings from Barna's broad base of research. Of course, there are always limitations to social research. But having data, instead of guessing, at least gives us a benchmark from which to understand how young people think, act, and feel. For the purposes of this chapter, I'm using a variety of different research studies that come from Barna, including *Faith for Exiles*, a book I wrote with Mark Matlock, *Gen Z*, volume 2, and a broad study we conducted with World Vision titled *The Connected Generation*, in which we interviewed more than fifteen thousand young people, ages eighteen to thirty-five, in twenty-five countries.

MENTORING SCREENAGERS

We're learning about the need for a new mindset for the formation practices of developing young people who are courageous, have convictions, and can live out their faith principles in real life. As you'll read in the pages that follow, mentoring is a vital component in helping young people grow in their faith.

We need a new vision and then a set of practices for mentoring, because so many other ways of human formation are diminishing in their efficacy. As my good friend author Andy Crouch observed recently, the kinds of institutions and places in which human beings are formed—households, schools, and faith communities—are losing their ability to form people.

This is, in large part, because we live in a screen age. Digital tools give us 24/7 access to information. The screens in our pockets and in our homes are all-pervasive. Like it or not, screens have become modern-day mentors, standing in for parents, teachers, coaches, youth pastors—all the people who historically have helped to guide and shape the actions and beliefs of the next generation.

Today we're living in a digital Babylon, a world of screens and online authority so all-encompassing that it's changing the way we think about what counts for a meaningful life and the plausibility of faith. Millennials and Gen Z are being discipled and mentored by Google and social media. They've come to trust information from the internet more than from institutions such as school, church, faith-based ministries, and other community-centered organizations and activities we've relied on to shape and guide their thinking. These institutions are losing their potency.

Digital Babylon requires a different way of discipling and educating young adults. We need better tools for forming human beings. But before we dive into ways to forge these new tools, it's helpful to get a picture of the hallmarks of Gen Z.

A PROFILE OF GEN Z

Young people are often accused of being unmotivated. Our Gen Z data debunks this and many other myths. We conducted fifteen hundred interviews with thirteen- to twenty-year-olds. When asked about their perceptions of success and hopes for the future, 65 percent say they agree strongly that they hope to achieve a lot in the next ten years. A full 74 percent agree with the statement, "My perspective on life tends to be positive." As many as 77 percent agree with the statement, "I've been successful in my life so far."

Underlying this overall positivity lurks an uncertainty about life. In response to the statement, "I tend to expect the worst to happen," 56 percent agree, while 44 percent say they either disagree somewhat or disagree strongly. These are just a few of the data points that help to paint a profile of the mindset of today's young people when it comes to their hopes and dreams for the future.

We also looked at a range of attitudes related to Gen Z's views on intergenerational relationships. A majority agree strongly or somewhat with these statements:

- I feel valued by the people in my life who are older than me.
- Older people don't seem to understand the pressures my generation is under.
- Those in positions of authority in my life have my best interests in mind.
- I often look at those who are older than me for advice when I need to make difficult decisions.
- I welcome positive criticism from those who are older than me.

They are less likely to agree with these statements:

- I mainly trust people my own age for insights and advice.
- It's hard for me to feel present with people.
- I meet regularly with someone who is a mentor to me. (Only 14 percent of Gen Z says this is true for them, 30 percent say this is somewhat true, 24 percent say they disagree strongly that they meet

regularly with a mentor. Only 11 percent strongly agree that they "meet regularly with someone whom I mentor.")

This shows us one of the obstacles on the road to developing better mentoring pathways: mentoring is not, as yet, a familiar part of the youth and young adult development ecosystem. It's always easier to help people do and improve things they're already doing than it is to have people start from scratch. Mentoring is an effective way to foster the faith of young people, but if it's not part of a church or academic institution's culture or programming, it's unlikely to serve as a viable path to spiritual formation. In this chapter, I hope to make a compelling case for why mentoring is worth implementing with your younger colleagues in academe.

CHURCH DROPOUTS

The loss of faith among young people should be a major catalyst for considering mentoring pathways. When I wrote *You Lost Me* in 2010, the percentage of young people who grew up Christian and ended up walking away from their faith community or from their faith entirely was 11 percent. Today, a decade later, that percentage has doubled. Now 22 percent of people ages thirteen to twenty walk away from their faith.

Within the Christian community in general and in Christian education in particular, the goal is to help form people into the image of Christ. With the surging percentage of young adults leaving the faith, we must take an honest and sober look at the fact that what we're doing to help form people spiritually isn't working as well as we hope.

The dropout of faith and of regular church community is one thing that's at stake; the moral and spiritual development, the kind of life we live for the sake of others, is another. There's also a whole range of practical things about relational and emotional health, a sense of who we are, and who we're becoming.

"I OFTEN FEEL . . ."

From our research for *The Connected Generation*, we gathered data on the emotional perspectives of young adults around the world. Though we conducted this research in 2019 before the pandemic, young adults' responses to "I often feel . . ." statements help create a useful emotional portrait of young adults.

Positive perspectives. "I often feel . . .":

- deeply cared for by those who were around me. (Only 33 percent of young adults around the globe, ages 18-35, feel this is true; the number is higher, at 36 percent, in the United States.)
- someone believes in me. (Again, only one-third say this is true.)
- satisfied with my life choices. (29 percent globally)
- secure in who I am. (28 percent)
- optimistic about the future. (40 percent)
- able to accomplish my goals. (34 percent)

Negative perceptions. Conversely, young adults, especially in the United States, say they "often feel":

- uncertain about the future. (40 percent global; 49 percent US)
- unable to do what I want. (27 percent global; 35 percent US)

They feel pressured . . .

- to be successful. (36 percent global; 42 percent US)
- to be perfect. (30 percent global; 33 percent US)
- by a parent's expectations. (17 percent global; 19 percent US)

They're anxious about important decisions and afraid to fail (40 percent global; 49 percent US), insecure (22 percent global; 30 percent US), sad or depressed (28 percent global; 39 percent US), and lonely and isolated from others (24 percent global; 34 percent US). About a quarter of young people worldwide feel that there are not enough opportunities available to them.

To some extent, every generation faces these same pressures. Because of the power of screens, however, today's young adults—the connected generation—face a deeper set of problems, and life for them raises epistemological questions of the plausibility of faith: Did Jesus really live? Is there a better way to think about this? Is Christianity the only way? Sounds a little like the seminal question posed in Genesis: Did God really say not to eat from any tree in the garden?

GOOGLE AND THE SEARCH FOR A MENTOR

Mentoring is so important for another reason: the manner in which young people find wisdom—answers to age-old questions about where to find truth and meaning—has changed; it's shifting to a digital and algorithmic source. In the past, sage adults and trusted leaders in our homes, schools, and churches may have been the people and places young people looked for guidance. Now the first responder for advice on love and life is Google—a faceless, disinterested search engine, hardly qualified to serve as a mentor to a generation of teens and young adults.

And yet who can blame them for seeking answers on the internet? Three important staples of society where young people can be formed—households, schools, and churches—have weakened in their potency. If we wish to restore these institutions so they can reclaim their relevance and power in guiding the next generation into adulthood, we must prioritize mentorship as a critical factor. We must find a better way forward or risk losing many among the next generation.

MENTORING TO MEET PRESSING NEEDS

Developing mentoring solutions is a crucial way forward, enabling those who care about the next generation to address young adults' most pressing questions and needs. There are five ways that developing more robust mentoring pathways could benefit young people. The first relates to teenagers' and young adults' mental health.

Mentoring solutions for mental health. Mental health issues rate high on the list of demanding topics in society, especially among emerging generations and within the church and schools. Data on Gen Z show that those in this age group are under pressure: an estimated 31 percent always or usually feel pressure to be successful or a need to be perfect. Roughly a quarter of Gen Z youth say they're externally pressured; they always or usually feel judged by older generations or pressured by parents' expectations. A quarter qualify as anxious; they always or usually feel afraid to fail, anxious about important decisions, and uncertain about the future. Conversely, 25 percent feel empowered, saying they always or usually feel

- "able to accomplish my goals,"
- "satisfied with my life choices,"
- "someone believes in me,"
- "prepared for everyday life,"
- "optimistic at the future," or
- "deeply cared for by those around me."

So, when they're feeling anxious, what do young people turn to for relief? Music and talking with someone are the two most common ways Gen Z respondents say they relieve anxiety. Watching videos, movies, and TV; meditating; sleeping; gaming; and physical activity are other ways they de-stress.

When they're lonely, 45 percent say they look to a person other than a family member for connection. A significantly lower percent of young adults (20 percent) connect with family, and 18 percent use music to fill the loneliness. Social media, gaming, and other technology show up in their responses to anxiety and to loneliness. It's not inherently wrong to do this, but it does reveal the degree to which screens serve as a proxy for real-life connection.

Mentoring solutions for trauma. Mentoring also provides a way to address the significant traumas that Gen Zers in the United States say they have experienced in their young lives. Here is a statistical snapshot of their pain:

- the death of a loved one (35 percent)
- suicidal thoughts (30 percent)
- betrayal by a loved one or someone you trusted (25 percent)
- racial discrimination (17 percent overall; 8 percent among Whites, 33 percent among young Blacks, 25 percent among Hispanics, 19 percent among Asians)
- domestic violence (16 percent)
- addiction (15 percent)
- divorce (15 percent)
- abuse and near-death experience or significant injuries, such as from an accidental shooting (13 percent)

- watching someone die or being abused (12 percent)
- job loss (10 percent)
- not having enough food, clothing, or shelter (9 percent)
- natural disaster (8 percent)
- major financial setback (7 percent)
- prisoner incarceration (6 percent)
- burglary or robbery (5 percent)
- conflicts, such as wars, bombings, or other types of attacks (5 percent)
- homicide and murder (4 percent)

Although these percentages decrease in this list of traumas, even the single-digit statistics from our sampling represent huge numbers of people in an absolute sense among the broader population of young people. It's also quite likely that some of these traumas are even more widespread than reported. Available social statistics on divorce, for instance, would indicate that a much larger percentage of teens in our country have felt the effects personally.

Our data offers one way of estimating the prevalence of trauma. At the very least, the range of traumatic experience suffered by young people indicates the significant part mentoring could play in providing a helpful buffer and healing path forward. Caring adults could serve as a key resource before, during, and after someone is exposed to or endures trauma.

We're seeing some positive trends among Millennials and Gen Zers, compared to older generations, in terms of their ability to identify and talk about mental health issues and deal with trauma. Helpfully, younger generations are especially open about their experiences. Comparing our research over twenty-five years, there's now less resistance to polling people about these kinds of questions. They don't seem to feel shame or apprehension about discussing these issues but, rather, seem willing to express their concerns.

Mentoring toward vocational discipleship. A third benefit of implementing mentoring is for its value as *vocational discipleship.* Vocational discipleship involves helping to shape young people in the way of Jesus to identify a work-related calling and then helping them be equipped and prepared for that kind of vocation, not necessarily in Christian ministry but across all career options, including the academic vocation. Colleges and universities can offer both the facility space and the mentors to walk alongside young adults who are trying to identify and live out their callings. Mentoring is a key catalyzing agent for vocational discipleship and an essential part of what students should experience during their college years both at school and in their church.

According to data from *The Connected Generation*, 60 percent of young adult Christians in the United States say, "My church has helped me better understand my purpose in life."

In my book with Mark Matlock, *Faith for Exiles*, we gained even deeper insight into this cohort of Christian young adults, whom we call *resilient disciples*. Resilient disciples are a statistically small but mighty group of young adults who self-identify as deeply committed Christians. We define *resilient disciples* as Christ followers who

1. attend church regularly and engage with their church more than just attending worship services,

2. trust firmly in the authority of the Bible,

3. are committed to Jesus personally and affirm he was crucified and raised from the dead to conquer sin and death, and

4. express desire to transform society as an expression of their faith.

Resilient disciples are more likely to say that their church influenced them vocationally. Here's a snapshot of how they responded to statements about their church's role in vocational discipleship:

- I'm given real chances to contribute to my church. (65 percent)
- I've learned what it feels like to be part of a team at church. (63 percent)
- At church, I've learned how the Bible applies to my field or interest area. (58 percent)
- My church has helped me to better live out my faith in the workplace. (64 percent)
- I have been inspired to live generously based on the example of people in my church. (58 percent)

Young adults are trying to sort out their life purpose through vocation—and more. They're looking for people to inspire them to live with Christian conviction, even when it comes to stewardship and generosity.

Colleges and universities can play a significant role in helping to shape a sense of calling, and they can learn effective ways to do this based on what we're learning from churches. Here are some of the ways resilient disciples say their church has helped shape their sense of calling:

- I have received helpful input from a pastor or church worker about my education. (43 percent)
- I became friends with someone who has helped guide my professional development. (40 percent)
- I received guidance on what schools or colleges to attend. (28 percent)
- I have access to leadership training for my job through my church. (25 percent)
- I have received a scholarship for college through my church. (13 percent)

The last two items are not frequently mentioned, but they represent ways that churches and places of learning could build young lives in practical, tangible ways. There's a real opportunity for the local church and higher education to increase their support of young adults and to develop intentional pathways for mentoring students in their faith and in their life and vocational choices.

At Barna we're passionate about vocational discipleship. We see it as an untapped pathway for discipleship for the church and in schools. In *Faith for Exiles*, we asked Christian teenagers what kinds of careers they were interested in. We took all of their open-ended responses and coded them into three major categories—entrepreneurial, science-minded, or creative careers. We found that about half of young Christian teens were interested in entrepreneurial careers; half were interested in science-minded careers; and one-third were interested in creative work.

This data gives church leaders and Christian educators an important window into the kinds of vocational mentors and educational programs young people need. We need enough entrepreneurial mentors for entrepreneurial-minded young people as much as we need science-minded mentors and creative mentors.

My friend Skye Jethani has written a lot about work and opportunities for the church to be at the center of vocational discipleship. Skye observes how, in the book of Genesis, God designs work for at least three different outcomes: to produce abundance, to develop order, and to cultivate beauty. Curious about the correlation between the outcomes of work and young people's career aspirations, we created a graphic with two sets of over-lapping circles—one featuring our three key vocational categories, entre-preneurial, science, and creative, and the other marked abundance, order, and beauty. A virtuous cycle clearly emerges whereby entrepreneurial careers generate abundance. With mentoring, entrepreneurs with abun-dance can bring order (processes and systems to start-ups), which leads to creating beauty (new ventures), which cultivates more opportunities for creating abundance in the world.

Through mentoring, science-minded young people can better under-stand God's design or order. You want your oncologist to understand the "decision trees" related to the medical field they're in, for instance. And you want your accountant to understand tax codes and engineers to under-stand structural loads for materials as they're building bridges and buildings. So science-minded young people could be mentored into the way of order.

And finally, creative careers are oriented toward beauty. The work of creative people reflects the glory of God in myriad ways that can be fos-tered and encouraged by mentors who see the impulse in young people to make the world more beautiful.

Although Christians believe that God's perfect kingdom is coming, we experience the curse of work in the thorns and thistles of sin. None-theless, we believe that Christ will return and perfect the work of our hands. Meanwhile, we can mentor young people into a vision of flour-ishing that includes teaching about careers that grow in abundance, order, and beauty.

It's clear that schools can have a deep impact on helping young adults gain clarity on issues of identity and vocation. By prioritizing vocational discipleship, higher education institutions will have a direct on-ramp to providing meaningful, relevant guidance and mentoring opportunities to young adults.

Instead of fostering self-interest and ambition, vocational mentoring flows from a belief that each person is created in the image of God with a divine destiny and a job to do—a vocation—and the place to find this is within the community of saints.

Relational mentoring. A fourth way for learning institutions to provide mentoring involves relational discipleship. College and university leaders can learn a lot about how to cultivate deeper relationships with students based on our research about how young people say they experience their local church.

Our work at Barna shows that young people are often experiencing a kind of church that is overly programmatic and oriented toward growing local church communities. They see churches as effective in fulfilling their own missions, but not necessarily in growing souls and growing people in the way of Jesus. It's almost as if we're more interested in building effective local institutions than we are in forming young people and discipling them in their faith.

In our research, here are some of the things Gen Z churchgoers say they experience in church:

- My faith motivates me to make a difference in the world. (34 percent agree strongly; 75 percent agree strongly or somewhat)
- I am satisfied with my Christian church community. (33 percent agree strongly)
- I have learned what it feels like to be part of a team at church. (31 percent agree strongly)
- I am given real chances to contribute to my church. (28 percent agree strongly)
- I am excited by the mission of the church in today's world. (27 percent agree strongly)
- I don't have as many close friends at church as I wish I had. (23 percent agree strongly; 58 percent agree somewhat)

Emotional climate of the church. In *Faith for Exiles*, we looked at how young adults form meaningful relationships at church, which defines, in large part, the emotional climate of the church. In each of the data points below, you'll see the critical role the church has played in building meaningful relationships with resilient disciples:

- The church is a place where I feel I belong. (88 percent)
- There is someone in my life who encourages me to grow spiritually. (85 percent)
- When growing up, I had close personal friends who were adults from my church. (77 percent)
- I admire the faith of my parents. (72 percent)
- I feel emotionally close to someone at my church. (64 percent)

This last data point is a good indicator of both the potential of mentoring and how lacking emotional connection often is in churches and likely at colleges and universities too. Habitual churchgoers (attend church but aren't deeply engaged), nomads/unchurched (self-identify as Christian but are no longer involved in a church), and prodigals/ex-Christians (grew up Christian but say they're no longer Christian) are the least likely to say they feel a warm connection to the church. This indicates a big relational gap within churches but also an opportunity for churches to focus on cultivating an emotional climate. Schools, too, have an opportunity to foster meaningful relationships with students to help them gain a sense of belonging and emotional connection with someone who cares deeply for them. Would that every school could become a place where all would say, *I feel I belong. I'm connected to a community of Christians. I feel emotionally close to someone.*

Resilient disciples. One of the fascinating things we learned in our research is about the interplay between resilient disciples and intergenerational relationships. Resilient disciples who have intergenerational relationships are much more likely to say they're satisfied with their church community (94 percent) compared to 81 percent of habitual churchgoers and only 69 percent of nomads.

When asked to rate the statement, "I meet regularly with someone who is a mentor to me," 70 percent of resilient disciples agreed compared with only 49 percent of habitual churchgoers and 45 percent for nomads. In our research for *Faith for Exiles*, we found that resilient disciples were much more likely to have strong, robust relationships. We asked a whole set of questions around relational health and well-being, such as the following: I have at least one close friend I trust with my secrets. When growing up, I had close personal friends who were adults. I have someone in my life other than family I can go to for advice on personal issues. My friends help me to be a better person. I have friends and family who are honest with me about my weaknesses. I am very content when I am by myself. I wish I had more close friendships.

For every one of these statements, resilient disciples are head and shoulders above the other three groups when it comes to relational outcomes. Interestingly, habitual churchgoers barely rate much higher than nomads and prodigals in terms of their positive relationships at church.

And so we have to ask ourselves, why is there this difference? Social research is unable to tell us much about cause and effect, but it does give us some indication that resilient disciples (whom we define based on their beliefs and their religious activities) are finding a type of relational connectedness in and among their lives. That's a powerful finding. It demonstrates that there is potential in mentoring and relational connectedness in and through a faith community. This same dynamic can happen in our colleges and universities too. When those bonds are strong, they help to propel positive outcomes among young people; they're setting goals and meeting them. After all, this is the kind of profile we all would want in our friendships and the kind of young people we want to grow and develop in our homes, schools, and churches.

One final comment on relational mentoring: we define meaningful relationships as being devoted to fellow believers we want to be around and want to emulate. Mentoring has the power to unlock that kind of potential, which is a profound opportunity. I look forward to seeing Christian colleges and universities turning their attention to creating this kind of relational output.

Instead of loneliness and isolation and some of the challenges of comparison brought on by social media, meaningful relationships matter.

College can become a place where young people like hanging out with other Christians—people who can shape them into who they're meant to be.

Cultivating contributors instead of consumers. The fifth outcome for mentoring can take place as learning institutions organize around common causes, helping young people become contributors, not merely consumers. The most effective churches and social organizations involve people in their mission.

One of the themes we explored in *Faith for Exiles* is how churches contribute to countercultural missions and the impact this has in cultivating resilient disciples. Our data show the ways churches stoke compassion in resilient disciples. These same opportunities exist in places of higher education:

- I better understand the needs of the poor. (65 percent)
- I had the opportunity to serve the poor in my community. (58 percent)
- I found a cause or issue that I'm passionate about. (53 percent)
- I better understand what is happening for the poor globally. (50 percent)
- I better understand social justice. (44 percent)
- I better understand the needs of marginalized people. (37 percent)
- I am given real opportunities to contribute. (73 percent)
- I have learned what it feels like to be part of a team. (57 percent)
- I have access to ministry training for ministry through my church. (48 percent)

These are many of the same kinds of questions we asked of global and US young adults in our study titled *The Connected Generation*. It's encouraging to see that about a third to a quarter of Christian young adults said that their churches had served as a place of both formation and activation, but those numbers could be much higher. Colleges and universities have a ripe opportunity to cultivate hearts and minds that are bent toward justice and initiatives that serve the common good. Mentoring in its highest form happens when we help young adults move from being consumers to contributing members of society, when we help them learn that they're blessed to be a blessing.

Mentoring helps people understand their place in the world and how a life well lived isn't just about achieving success, making the grades, hitting all the marks; it's about giving back to society. As an antidote to entitlement, being part of a countercultural mission helps people experience a positive sense of identity and an understanding of the larger human story. Our lives are meant to be organized around something larger than ourselves, and this is what every person, and especially every young person, is looking for.

CATALYZING A CULTURE OF MENTORSHIP

Mentoring can be a key catalyzing agent for helping young people grow into who they're meant to be in the world. Unfortunately, churches, schools, and households are increasingly ineffective at cultivating relationships and emotional climates in which relationships can thrive. We need more life-on-life efforts like mentoring to answer some of the big pressures prevalent today: the search for identity, anxiety and loneliness, driving ambition, and entitlement. With mentoring, there is a way forward to help people identify as followers of Christ and children of God, to realize that the Christian Scriptures provide relevant wisdom even today. Open the book of Ecclesiastes and the other Wisdom literature to find a bedrock of wisdom that can help discern how to proceed on a faithful life path.

MEASURING SUCCESS

How can colleges and universities measure their success in mentoring young people? We can return to some of the previously cited data about Gen Z. In fact, asking young people to rate how much they agree with these statements (agree strongly; agree somewhat; disagree somewhat; disagree strongly) can give a way to measure the impact of mentoring efforts, whether it be in schools, church communities and clubs, or even in one's household.

Ask your student body to provide either qualitative or quantitative input on the following statements:

- I feel valued by the people in my life who are older than me.
- Older people don't seem to understand the pressures my generation is under.
- Those in positions of authority in my life have my best interests in mind.
- I often look to those who are older than me for advice when I need to make difficult decisions.
- I welcome positive criticism from those who are older than me.
- I mainly trust people my own age for insights and advice.
- It's hard for me to feel present with people.
- I meet regularly with someone who is a mentor to me. (This one, in particular, could be a key metric of success.)
- I meet regularly with someone whom I mentor. (A healthy mentoring culture will instill a value to be mentored as much as to mentor others.)

There are so many compelling reasons to institute mentoring in our schools, churches, and communities. Though it can be hard to get it off the ground and you'll confront obstacles—people are busy, they don't think they have the abilities and/or time, or they just have never mentored before—there's so much opportunity.

Even in Scripture, we see how Jesus chose his disciples to mentor them. In fact, the real lasting impact of Jesus's life on earth was through the relationships with those who were closest to him. Perhaps we've relied too heavily on mechanisms that attempt to mass-produce disciples. We've created this sort of automated approach, and yet there's so much to be gained for the Christian community to come alongside young people in a life-on-life manner and provide this kind of meaningful, catalyzing agent in the form of mentoring.

Mentoring matters. It's time for the church and agents into which it breathes life, such as colleges and universities, to rediscover this crucial formation process.

2

LEADING INTEGRATED LIVES

*Navigating Personal and Professional Commitments
Through Mentorship*

TIM CLYDESDALE

"Thanks a lot!" "Yeah, I really appreciate it!" At first glance, this reads as positive, even effusive. But do this: read both quotes again, infusing each with as much young adult sarcasm and eye-rolling as you can muster. Now you will hear them as I did, from the mouths of a half-dozen undergraduate research assistants, during a weekly project meeting a decade ago. So why, you might ask, were these assistants feeling so "grateful"? Some background is in order. We were a few weeks into the semester, and these sophomores and juniors had spent the first weeks reading background material about emerging adulthood and had now begun to code interviews with other college students and recent alums, conducted during field site research for my book *The Purposeful Graduate: Why Colleges Must Talk to Students About Vocation*.[1]

"Thanks to this class, I now have a label for what I've been feeling," said one assistant: "a quarter-life crisis! And apparently, it's contagious, because I told my sister about it, and she says she's having one too!" In time, I came to understand such reactions as a pass-through effect, more commonly reported to me by faculty and staff involved with their campus's vocational exploration initiatives who discovered that engaging vocational questions was as relevant to them as it was to the undergraduate targets of the

---

[1]Tim Clydesdale, *The Purposeful Graduate: Why Colleges Must Talk to Students About Vocation* (Chicago: University of Chicago Press, 2015).

initiative. At that moment, however, I wasn't sure what to say in response to these humorously expressed "complaints," because I had not designed this as a vocational exploration seminar but rather as a hands-on data analysis project for undergraduates interested in joining my research project. I think I said a few words about these being important questions worth taking time to consider and discuss with others, and then I refocused our attention on coding techniques—a classic dodge-and-redirect move by this unprepared professor. A decade later, though, I realize that what I designed as an undergraduate research experience had lasting effects on all six participants, with three obtaining doctorates and pursuing scholarly careers, another two completing degrees in education and teaching high school, and the remaining one completing a dual master's in public health and public policy and working at a health-policy think tank.

In hindsight, I see that this experience leveraged three essential components of effective vocational mentorship: reflection, practice, and community. Admittedly, the project did the least with reflection, as it introduced calling and vocation as life-shaping ideas but did not facilitate inward and outward reflection opportunities. (Inward vocational reflection involves an examination of one's interests, skills, and deep joys; outward vocational reflection requires an understanding of a world beyond the self that is vast, complex, and troubled.) Nevertheless, the project did involve a lot of practice, as we spent hours doing important work together. Serendipitously, those hours spent coding and writing in a common computer lab created community, which gave each student partners for reflection and practice.

PRIOR GLEANINGS

I wish I had identified these components of effective mentorship years ago, but it was the occasion of this Mentoring Matters Symposium and the attendant writing assignment that crystalized for me the role of reflection, practice, and community. Despite three decades of research on American teens and emerging adults, and a quarter-century of teaching and advising college students, I did not understand this clearly until now. That said, I can see the seeds of these components across previous scholarly inquiries.

For example, my research on high school graduates indicted American culture for its failure to convey to its adolescents the importance of thoughtful reflection on their lives and larger world.[2] My study of vocational exploration on college campuses led me to identify individualist and traditionalist cultural trajectories, which set hollow targets of private happiness and Lake Wobegon nostalgia, while pro-vocational campus communities produced graduates whose interdependent cultural trajectories demonstrated both joy and godly grit.[3] Most recently, I summarized American twentysomethings as postmodern pilgrims, struggling to navigate their journeys to adulthood, all the while leaving the maps and destination guides of faith communities unconsulted.[4] Across each of these inquiries, I now see abundant evidence for the contributions of reflection, practice, and community, along with the consequences of their absence.

Two examples should help to illustrate this. During research for *The Twentysomething Soul*, we interviewed Sahil, a premed student at an Ivy League university.[5] Sahil's mother, a physician, and his father, an engineer, emigrated from India in their 20s. Sahil was their only child, and they afforded him wide latitude to pursue his own path. Indeed, Sahil emphasized that his pursuit of medicine was his own choice, not undertaken out of obligation to his parents. To illustrate his freedom, he pointed to his rejection of his parents' Hinduism and how his parents were "perfectly fine" with his atheism. Sahil also boasted about living in a fraternity house and about his beautiful girlfriend with whom he spent most of his time. Our vision of Sahil and his girlfriend playing beer pong in a crowded fraternity basement was soon moderated, however, by Sahil's explanation that most of his fraternity brothers were heavily involved in Hillel, followed kosher food laws, and fasted "it seems very often," and that his "Indian premed girlfriend" spent "most of the time" studying, which Sahil did too.

---

[2] See especially Tim Clydesdale, *The First Year Out: Understanding American Teens After High School* (Chicago: University of Chicago Press, 2007), 199-200.

[3] See Clydesdale, *Purposeful Graduate*, 52-53, 219-23.

[4] See Tim Clydesdale and Kathleen Garces-Foley, "Practical Postmodernism," chap. 7 in *The Twentysomething Soul: Understanding the Religious and Secular Lives of American Young Adults* (New York: Oxford University Press, 2019).

[5] See Clydesdale, *Twentysomething*, 148-51.

What Sahil's life illustrates, then, is a studious variant of the individualist cultural trajectory, which defines the good life in terms of private accomplishment, intimacy, and accumulation. And when we caught up with Sahil at the end of his first year of medical school, his trajectory was unchanged—performing well in school remained his top priority, his (new) girlfriend was a med school classmate, his fasting Hillel fraternity brothers had been replaced by a graduate student roommate who kept to himself, and his housing was upgraded to a condo that his parents purchased for him. Sahil enjoyed a privileged life, which supported his prioritization of his medical education; I certainly commend him for taking his training seriously. At the same time, I see Sahil's life as narrowly constructed and devoid of both reflection and community engagement.

By contrast, during research for *The Purposeful Graduate*, we met Jeff, who like Sahil was a premed student and whose mother was a physician.[6] But that is where the similarity ends, as Jeff attended an evangelical college with vocational exploration programming. At college, Jeff quickly joined a spiritual mentorship group with six other male students and a faculty mentor. He also took wide advantage of his college's local and international service opportunities. These experiences confirmed his interest in becoming a medical missionary, but it was his junior-year involvement as a paid summer research assistant to a biology professor that led him to marry his long-standing interest in medical missions with the pursuit of medical research. In short, Jeff wanted to become an evangelical version of Dr. Paul Farmer, the physician-anthropologist who founded Partners in Health to combat antibiotic resistant tuberculosis in Haiti, while simultaneously publishing peer-reviewed research in infectious disease and medical anthropology. Combining career interests was not the only marriage on Jeff's mind, however. During our interview, he told us he was working on saving up for an engagement ring, which he would present to his college girlfriend after they graduated in the spring.

When we caught up with Jeff again, he was starting his second year of medical school and settling into an illegal basement apartment with his

---

[6]See Clydesdale, *Purposeful Graduate,* 15-20.

college-girlfriend-now-wife, after returning from an eight-week "honeymoon" doing medical missions together in Sri Lanka. It was not a real apartment, just a basement that a "really nice lady" rented out; keeping costs down would allow them to return "to the field" the next summer. As busy as his days were, Jeff was in no rush to get off the phone and seemed happy to speak to us. We asked how he managed to sound so relaxed, and he acknowledged that American life was "very busy, very loud, very on-the-go." But he explained how he'd been working to learn "principles in the Christian faith of silence and contemplation, social activism with a cause, but yet not making that such a busy process." Jeff was the picture of equanimity, content with his life despite its everyday challenges, and committed to a medical career in service to global needs. His self-reflectiveness and global engagement contrasted sharply with Sahil's. Both aspects reinforced the interdependent cultural trajectory that Jeff calibrated quite intentionally during college.

SUMMONED TO THEOLOGIZE

It may be tempting for evangelical readers to congratulate themselves as they read Jeff's story. That would be premature, however. Jeff's story is far from representative. Scores of interviews and conversations with evangelical young adults demonstrate not a prevalence of vocational reflection or intentionality, but rather a sanctification of dominant cultural trajectories and a fatalism about God's will. Let me explain. For new or immature Christians, the common pattern is to sprinkle sanctified terminology on the dominant cultural practices and patterns. American materialism is not questioned; rather, private happiness and accumulation becomes the blessed life, and Wobegon nostalgia becomes Christian nationalism. For young adult Christians more mature in their faith, there is a sincere desire to seek God's will but little beyond fatalism to discern it. An unexpected offer of an assistant manager position from Chick-fil-A is, for example, interpreted as God's will rather than continued pursuit of employment as a music teacher, despite possessing a bachelor of music education and sizable college loans.

I am neither a biblical scholar nor a theologian, but I will suggest a common weakness in folk evangelical theologies is the failure to recognize vocation's dual components: discernment and summoning. Discernment requires internal and external processes (referenced above) of honest self-reflection and humbling self-transcendence. Summoning involves obeying the call of God to work that clearly needs doing (e.g., caring for an ill family member, helping a needy neighbor). Together, discernment and summoning form a dual helix (like DNA), giving shape to vocation across our earthly decades. At times, attuned to our giftedness and skills, we pursue and apply ourselves to good work that brings us deep joy. At other times, heeding a summons that is patently clear, we care for our neighbor's special-needs child, *despite* our lack of giftedness with children, so that our neighbor can take her husband to chemotherapy. (Doing this brings deep joy, too, even as it is hard.) And most of the time, our days encompass a mix of discerned and summoned activity.

The error, then, that the Chick-fil-A assistant manager above makes is ignoring the discernment process, which turns his receptiveness to summoning into fatalism. His openness to God's summoning is not balanced by an understanding of God gifting him with musical and teaching talent. Which is not to say that for a spell, perhaps while his self-employed mother recuperates from an injury, this young man would be acting in good faith to accept the job offered and support his family financially. But as he does this, he must remember his giftedness too, keeping his music teaching skills honed (perhaps via volunteering with a children's music group) and his resume before school superintendents. Ignoring vocational discernment and failing to appreciate the freedom to deploy one's skills and talents joyfully is the most widespread mistake I encounter among evangelical youth.

But there is a parallel error that happens when young adults downplay or ignore the summoning component of vocation, which is to convert vocational discernment into a privilege. This is less common (but not rare) among evangelical young adults, as most evangelicals understand that affirming "Jesus is Lord" requires obedience to that same Lord. This error was most prevalent at the non-evangelical campuses I studied that hosted vocational exploration programming. Since these campuses were largely uncomfortable with the idea of a Caller who makes claims on one's life, they would frame calling as an internal voice, or as a calling from humanity-in-general, and therefore focus on self-reflection and service. The former devolved into a question of "How shall I bless the world *with me*?" and was rightly written off by some observers as another privilege that affluent young idealists got to enjoy. The latter would prompt, for many young adults, a sense of other-directed calling. The problem these young adults then confronted, due to the moral "whateverism"[7] dominant among American emerging adults, was the absence of a way to articulate their vocational call in ethically significant ways. They might choose to dedicate themselves to fighting sexual trafficking, for example, but have only their personal preference and individual happiness as bases to explain their dedication. Later, if their dedication were to shift to opening a pizza franchise, they would have no basis to question either the moral significance of fast food or a life so oriented.

Effective mentoring needs to help young adults appreciate vocation as both reflection and summoning. This is especially important when the vocation is academic, given the lack of hospitality toward religious and spiritual devotion encountered in most doctoral and postdoctoral programs. The most persuasive way to do this, I observed, was not didactic but rather a far more compelling tack: narrative. Mentors would share their own academic vocation stories of summoning and of reflection. They would solicit the stories of others framed in the same ways. They would help mentees narrate their past summonses (heeded and ignored) and previous reflections (honest and less so). And they would facilitate their doing so with academically like-minded peers. A healthy, pro-vocational academic community would include both mentors and peers, all of whom used a common vocabulary of vocation and had access to a common library of vocational stories. Mentors and mentees alike found membership in such an academic community to be transformative.

MESSY YET JOYFUL

In *The Twentysomething Soul*, I described four strategies that American twentysomethings settle into with respect to religion and spirituality: they

---

[7]See Christian Smith, "Morality Adrift," chap. 1 in *Lost in Transition: The Dark Side of Emerging Adulthood* (New York: Oxford University Press, 2011).

prioritize it, reject it, sideline it, or innovate it. The eclectic religiosity of the latter is least common. The dominant pattern (even among evangelical twentysomethings) is to sideline faith and spiritual life; that is, to neither reject it nor prioritize it, but to keep it nominally a part of their lives until some future moment when they would "get serious" about it. Similarly, the dominant pattern among religiously unaffiliated twentysomethings is to approach their nonaffiliation with indifference; that is, to not think about their nonreligious identity, to not reflect on their moral views, and to not ponder their spirituality. The priorities of most twentysomethings center instead on everyday adult life—juggling work, friendships, finances, and intimacy. By keeping religious and secular identities to the side, they believe that they can juggle better.

Such a strategy certainly characterized Sahil's life, as he regarded his hands plenty full with his medical education and girlfriend. Sahil was "more or less satisfied" with his medical schooling, and guardedly optimistic about a new romance, which is better than many younger twentysomethings can report. But his answers to our "life satisfaction index" questions revealed his doubts about choosing the "right school" for medical education, even as he was performing well academically, along with his view that had he chosen a different school he would have "been closer" to his previous girlfriend, and "maybe [the breakup] wouldn't have happened." Sahil did say he was happy with his financial life and living arrangements, but it took longer to find friends in medical school since "almost 50% of the class is from the undergrad school . . . and never really opened up to anyone else." Eventually Sahil connected with other out-of-state students, which made his social life "satisfactory" by the end of his first year. Finally, Sahil told us that he had no religious or spiritual life and was satisfied with its absence. Overall Sahil was more satisfied than dissatisfied with his life, and he netted a moderate score on our life satisfaction index.

By contrast, Jeff's life satisfaction score was high. He was "very much" satisfied with his medical schooling. Although his finances and living arrangements were obviously lower than Sahil's, Jeff said he was "very blessed financially" to be sharing "a small basement with my wife." Jeff's social life "is my wife [laughing]—we're trying to branch out." But "I consider myself a pretty sociable guy, [and] I made some really close friends last year." Satisfied with his social life, he reported that his married life was "awesome." Our last question asked about Jeff's satisfaction with religious and spiritual life. Jeff went deep, talking at length about his conversations with his spiritual mentor, reporting that "I've never been more calm and patient" due to "my belief in God and my faith." Jeff's answers not only converted to a high score on our life satisfaction index, but they also gave us a rich sense of his life's weekly rhythm, daily challenges, and lasting joys.

Comparing the two interviews, I found Sahil to be gracious in his manners and honest in his responses to our questions. I was certainly grateful that he took the time to speak with us. What Sahil's interview did, though, was provide us with an update—a report, if you will—on his life. Jeff's interview was likewise gracious and honest, but his interview ran 33 percent longer than Sahil's and was marked by a much wider emotional range, from laughter to contemplation to an intimate recounting of a bout of insomnia and how he overcame it. What Jeff's interview did was invite us into the messy yet joyful busyness of his life and provide us with a nuanced understanding of his external and internal world as he experienced these on a daily basis.

Sahil and Jeff were 2 of 123 respondents to the life satisfaction index. I report on this in *The Purposeful Graduate*, statistically comparing those who participated in vocational exploration programming as undergraduates with those who did not participate.[8] With a scale that ran from -6 to +6, nonparticipants had a median life satisfaction score of 1.8, while participants in vocational exploration had a median score of 4.9. And these differences persisted even after adding statistical controls for age, gender, race, and parental socioeconomic status. Vocational exploration during college boosts postcollegiate life satisfaction regardless of age, sex, race, ethnicity, or parental social class.

Three things stand out most from these analyses. First, when undergraduates engage in vocational reflection and exploration, the effects

---

[8]See Clydesdale, *Purposeful Graduate*, 121-25.

are palpable even one year after graduation. When I contrast that with how little students recall from their college course work just three months later, this demonstrates that vocational exploration has impressive staying power. Second, the magnitude of the difference in life satisfaction is striking. Nonparticipants are "more or less satisfied," to quote Sahil, with life after college, while participants in vocational exploration programs are overwhelmingly satisfied with their lives. It is the difference between living and what positive psychologists call "flourishing." Third, when I added a measure of participation in worship to these statistical analyses, I discovered that congregational involvement combined with vocational exploration explains 43 percent of the overall variation in respondents' life satisfaction scores. That is, twentysomethings who engaged in vocational exploration as undergraduates and now attend worship regularly report substantially higher life satisfaction than peers who did not engage in vocational exploration or who do not attend worship regularly. Why? I argue that "vocational exploration produces a pattern of examined living," while "regular participation in congregation worship reinforces that pattern and encourages positive engagement with others."[9]

These are remarkable results, but I find them a bit antiseptic in their description. Tracy Turner, a military brat *and* preacher's kid whom I met during research for *The Purposeful Graduate*, summed up the above analyses more memorably than I could. During her interview one year after graduating from college—said interview taking place as she was sitting in the dining room of a dilapidated manse that she and five other recent graduates were using as a base for urban volunteer ministry—she elaborated on her answers to our life satisfaction questions: "I feel good about the quality of life I lead, and I think that I have a life that is centered in faith, but [laughing]—I am also just out of college, I live in a household of postcollege friends and there's wine!"[10] And sharing Tracy's joie de vivre, we laughed too.

---

[9]Clydesdale, *Purposeful Graduate*, 124.
[10]Clydesdale, *Purposeful Graduate*, 121.

GENERATION, SMEDGERATION . . .

Up to now, I have focused on the three ingredients for successful, vocational mentoring: reflection, practice, and community. These apply to any vocation, to be sure, but are pivotal for academic vocational mentoring. Academic mentors, and any who aspire to foster meaningful mentorship, are advised to leverage these three ingredients widely. But I would be remiss if I ended this chapter now, without addressing an egregious error that clouds much writing and thinking about faith and young adults: generational theorizing. That is, claims about birth cohorts that start like this: Millennials are this, Gen Z is that, iGen wants this, the lost gen hates that. Such claims are as useful, and as scientifically rooted, as daily horoscopes.

The father, if you will, of generational theory was German sociologist Karl Mannheim (1893–1947).[11] Mannheim's *Ideology and Utopia* investigated how it was that wholly distinct worldviews could arise and be maintained concurrently by geographically overlapping subgroups. His specific focus was utopian social movements, of which there were no shortage during his research in Europe. Mannheim identified *three* primary causes of these movements: social class, location, and, most important for our purposes, generation. About the latter, Mannheim was the first to argue that a historic event or era could have a lasting and differentiating effect on a cohort, creating a generational consciousness. The crucial phrase in the previous sentence, however, is *could have*—not will have, must have, or always has. Mannheim was precise about his claim of *potential* generational effects; the popular peddlers of generational theories that follow, however, have been careless.[12]

Making claims about change over time is, for social scientists whose work undergoes anonymous peer review, exceedingly difficult. That is because three (3!) broad categories of factors can influence how people change over time: change can occur because of age (i.e., maturation) effects, period (i.e., era) effects, or cohort (i.e., generation)—and often it is

---

[11]Karl Mannheim, *Ideology and Utopia* (Bonn: F. C. Cohen, 1929; London: Routledge, 1936).

[12]For a fuller discussion, see Eric Hoover, "The Millennial Muddle: How Stereotyping Students Became an Industry," *Chronicle of Higher Education*, October 11, 2009; Bobby Duffy, *The Generation Myth: Why When You're Born Matters Less Than You Think* (New York: Basic Books, 2021).

a tangle of all three. Untangling this Gordian knot is, for all intents, impossible due to any study's unmeasured variables and insufficient length of data collection.[13] But peddlers of generational theories are undeterred by insufficient data. They know book sales and hefty consulting fees await their generational stereotypes, and they'll be damned if they let accuracy or peer review stand in the way of their claims.

Take your pick, then, of generational labels these peddlers will sell you: there is the boomerang generation, iGen, generation 9-11, the Lost Generation, Millennials, Post-Millennials, Generation Me, the App Generation, the Dumbest Generation, and Gen X/Y/Z. With each label, you will find matching books, lectures, consultants, and tote bags. What you won't be able to match, though, are the birth years assigned to these labels: Gen X, for example, has been defined as those born between 1961 and 1981, 1964 and 1982, or 1966 and 1976, while Millennials may include those born between 1982 and 2004, 1983 and 2000, or 1977 and 1994. So don't try to comparison shop for generations, because sizing will be a problem: one peddler's Gen X cohort can be as small as eleven years while another's as roomy as twenty-one years. The years do not match because generation effects (if any) are deeply entwined with period effects. Was Y2K, 9-11, the Great Recession or the iPhone *profoundly* more influential on fifteen-year-olds than it was on thirty-five-year-olds or sixty-five-year-olds? I doubt it, and so do millions of octogenarian iPhone users. Similarly, can one confidently attribute a twenty-year-old's foolish decisions to social media consumption and not to age effects like insufficient life experience or one's still developing prefrontal cortex? A careful social scientist never makes such overblown, single-variable claims.

None of this is to deny the existence of real differences between the young and old, nor the possibility that a generation can form. But the former are most often functions of maturation and life course differentials,

---

[13]For an introduction to the scholarly literature on age, period, and cohort effect research, see N. D. Glenn, "The Utility and Logic of Cohort Analysis," *Journal of Applied Behavioral Science* 17 (1981): 247-57; Yang Yang and Kenneth C. Land, "A Mixed Models Approach to the Age-Period-Cohort Analysis of Repeated Cross-Section Surveys, with an Application to Data on Trends in Verbal Test Scores," *Sociological Methodology* 36 (2006): 75-97; Andrew Bell and Kelvyn Jones, "The Impossibility of Separating Age, Period, and Cohort Effects," *Social Science & Medicine* 93 (September 2013): 163-65.

while the latter seems to require profoundly and pervasively influential events, such as the Great Depression or World War II, to forge a distinctive cohort outlook. My advice to readers who want to have better conversations across generations, to say nothing of mentorship, is to gather up their posters, books, and other generational miscellany and use them as kindling in their fireplaces and woodstoves this winter. That way, you'll get some value from the money that generational peddlers bilked from you.

UNDER THE SUN

Here's a truth you can carry with you: generations have far more in common than they have differences. Young adults want meaningful lives; so do older adults. Young adults want to make a difference through their work, enjoy companionship with their friends, and find love and tranquility in their homes; so do older adults. And those young adults considering academic vocations want to pursue scholarly projects that are important and valued; so do their older academic mentors. To be sure, the world is changing, and younger folks typically experience the leading edge of these changes sooner, but the desire for love, significance, and meaningful work transcends age.

Of course, none of this should come as a surprise to the readers of this volume, who hold as sacred truth that "there is nothing new under the sun" (Ecclesiastes 1:9). Nor should there be any surprise about the three levers of (academic, vocational) mentorship named in this chapter: reflection, practice, and community. These are ancient levers, in evidence since Abraham used them to ready Isaac to play his part in God's purposes. You can rest assured that reflection, practice and community can work as effectively now as they have across the millennia. And, hey, how about that—this chapter ends with a Millennial claim worth remembering!

3

CALL AND RESPONSE

Mentoring for Organizational Fit and Flourishing

MARGARET DIDDAMS

A vocational calling from God is always a call into community, creating mutual affirmation and reciprocal support among individuals and the organizations they inhabit. It's easy to picture this in the context of churches: a pastor has a sense of calling from God to the work of the pastorate and to a specific church. The church in turn calls its pastor to serve its congregation. During a pastor's tenure, there is a constant giving and receiving between the pastor and his or her ecclesia as they work together toward their mutual calling.

While one can grasp this mutuality and alignment of calling for pastors and their churches, it is no less true for academic institutions and their employees, even though this is not how we typically think about the academic vocation. The language used to describe God's *vocare*, his call on one's life, is often highly personal, with little attention given to the institution in which it will be lived. The lightly conceptualized context seems like a fuzzy background in a Zoom call. In conversations with student advisees, we often ask about their sense of calling to a particular type of work, role, or cause. We don't think twice when they respond in the first person about "my call" and how they see their work fitting into God's plan and providence. Although the topic of calling is a corrective to a material, self-oriented, and transactional view of work, it can often appear to be ethereal and not necessarily grounded in time and place, and amidst others. For example, two leading researchers in the area of work as a calling, Bryan Dik and Ryan Duffy, have conceptualized calling as

> a transcendent summons, experienced as originating beyond the self, to approach a particular life role in a manner oriented toward demonstrating or deriving a sense of purpose or meaningfulness and that holds other-oriented values and goals as primary sources of motivation.[1]

The emphasis here is on a personal sense of meaning and purpose, a very cognitive-heavy definition with a disembodied perspective. Not surprisingly, organizations in which people will live out this call, and the people with whom they will work and to whom they will report, are merely the context in which to derive a personal calling.

But God also calls organizations, whether churches, educational institutions, not-for-profits or more traditional commercial entities, to do the work of his kingdom.[2] It's not appropriate to think of bricks and mortar as being some sort of living entity that can commune with God. In fact, with many people working remotely for multiple years due to the pandemic, it's clear that organizations are not their buildings. As management scholar Benjamin Schneider famously wrote, "The people make the place."[3] Organizations are social structures that shape and maintain relationships among their members. No matter what an organization does, whether focused on its external outcomes of products, services, and care provided to customers, clients, students, or even parishioners, or focused on its internal processes of organizational charts, budgets, managers, teams, articulated strategies, workflows, acceptable methods of communication, and hallway interactions, they all have relationships at their core. Management scholars have shown for thirty years that an integrated approach to external outcomes and internal processes is necessary for organizational success.[4]

---

[1]Bryan J. Dik and Ryan D. Duffy, "Calling and Vocation at Work: Definitions and Prospects for Research and Practice," *Counseling Psychologist* 37, no. 3 (2009): 427.
[2]Jeffrey B. Van Duzer, *Why Business Matters to God (and What Still Needs to Be Fixed)* (Downers Grove, IL: IVP Academic, 2010).
[3]Benjamin Schneider, "The People Make the Place," *Personnel Psychology* 40, no. 3 (1987): 437-53.
[4]Thomas Donaldson and Lee E. Preston, "The Stakeholder Theory of the Corporation: Concepts, Evidence, and Implications," *Academy of Management Review* 20, no. 1 (1995): 65-91.

This is no less true for higher education. Although many college and university mission statements focus on the education of their students, the generation of original scholarship, and service to their communities, institutions might also articulate their internal missions: how they will live out their missions through values and goals directed toward employees. Baylor University does this succinctly in the last sentence of its mission statement. "The mission of Baylor University is to educate men and women for worldwide leadership and service by integrating academic excellence and Christian commitment within a caring community."[5] Likewise, the mission statement of my doctoral alma mater, NYU, puts a great deal of emphasis on its internal focus:

> New York University's mission is to be a top quality international center of scholarship, teaching and research. This involves retaining and attracting outstanding faculty who are leaders in their fields, encouraging them to create programs that draw outstanding students, and providing an intellectually rich environment. NYU seeks to take academic and cultural advantage of its location and to embrace diversity among faculty, staff and students to ensure a wide range of perspectives, including international perspectives, in the educational experience.[6]

An integrated approach for a Christian community means that the internal mission is seen as no less a calling from God, by which all community members have roles and responsibilities to cultivate work environments where the external mission can be carried out efficiently and effectively, resources are stewarded appropriately, toxicity is minimized, and each organizational entity is responsible to support the other for both individual and communal flourishing.[7] So, whether explicit or tacit, there is always a mutuality of call between individuals and their institutions, a reciprocal call and response. This mutuality is at the heart of organizational socialization. It is a joint process where all employees, especially newcomers, as they move from outsiders to insiders, are

---

[5]Baylor University, "Mission Statement," www.baylor.edu/about/index.php?id=88781.
[6]"NYU Mission Statement," www.nyu.edu/about.html.
[7]Margaret Diddams, "Good Work, Done Well and for the Right Reasons: Playing at Work," *Christian Scholar's Review* 50, no. 4 (2021): 423-34.

encouraged in ways that benefit the institutional mission and allow them to actively shape their organizations while experiencing meaningful work.[8] Baylor's "caring community" harkens back to Ernest Boyer's work on building community in institutions of higher education.[9] Boyer also noted this mutuality, writing that caring communities are "place[s] where the well-being of each member is sensitively supported and where service to others is encouraged."[10] He added that "a college is a humane enterprise and it is more than mere sentiment to suggest that its quality depends upon the heads and the hearts of the individuals in it."[11] Organizational socialization is more than onboarding new faculty. Done well, it is an investment in the intentional design of a vibrant academic and humane institution.

BACKGROUND

Baby Boomer faculty who joined the professorate as junior faculty in the 1980s and 1990s are likely to tell a common narrative regarding their organizational socialization: there was none. After running the gauntlet to prove their worthiness through the application and interview process and signing an employment contract that was lower than they had expected, they were given the most decrepit offices in the department, assigned to teach at least one intro section to hundreds of students (even though they likely received no training on pedagogy in graduate school), and expected to find the time to publish their recently defended dissertations. That was certainly my story as a newbie instructor at Columbia University, where I was grilled about attending Wheaton College (IL) as an undergraduate, assigned an oversized closet as an office, and taught a section of 125 students each semester.

---

[8]Van Maanen and Schein make the point that every time employees change jobs within an organization, some socialization is necessary for employee adjustment. John Van Maanen and Edgar H. Schein, "Toward a Theory of Organizational Socialization," *Research in Organizational Behavior* 1 (1979): 209-64.

[9]The Carnegie Foundation for the Advancement of Teaching, *Campus Life: In Search of Community*, foreword by Ernest L. Boyer (Princeton, NJ: The Carnegie Foundation for the Advancement of Teaching, 1990).

[10]Carnegie Foundation, *Campus Life*, 8.

[11]Carnegie Foundation, *Campus Life*, 54.

My experience was not unique among my graduate school peers as we started our academic careers. At one point, a friend who had landed a prestigious first appointment but also felt dropped on her head bemoaned, "It's byzantine, absolutely byzantine." The free-agent mindset of established faculty made it difficult to find someone to turn to for support, unless one was collaborating with a more senior person who could be helpful to make sure that this newly hired junior colleague was not overly burdened. As Christians we may not always embrace Darwinism, but, given my own horror stories and those I have heard from older faculty, "the survival of the fittest," even at Christian institutions, too often has been the unstated modus operandi.

But, happily, four interrelated events shifted that model for new faculty with the turn of the millennium. First, the scholarship of teaching and learning was gaining momentum with new national and international or-ganizations, conferences, and journals. Teaching and student learning were no longer relegated to an art form that was to be uniquely shaped by each professor. Faculty could receive training on empirically validated suc-cessful teaching strategies tied to student learning. Second, regional ac-creditation agencies wanted institutions to show evidence of student out-comes. Were students learning what we said we were teaching them? Were institutions who said they shaped character actually doing so? Third, with the 2008 recession, state legislatures also wanted accountability that state funds were being used appropriately to educate in-state students. Finally, every institution was spending millions on technology for faculty and their classrooms. How was that technology being used to maximize learning? How could it be used? What training, especially for new faculty, was being offered on technology? Each of these created not only a new need for ac-countability but attention to how new faculty members were being brought on board.

As Christian institutions grew throughout the same period, more Christian faculty members were being hired who had not attended Christian institutions of higher education, so they had not been socialized into what was expected of them in the classroom, nor did they necessarily have the depth of theological and biblical understanding to create and

deliver Christ-centered curriculum. This too has required Christian institutions to be more intentional about developing socialization programs for
new faculty. With all these pressures, most institutions, Christian and
otherwise, have created centers for faculty development over the past
20 years; such centers have played an important role in moving institutions
away from "eating their young" to having a point person whose responsibility is new faculty flourishing.

After sixteen years in the professorate, I served as the director of Seattle
Pacific University's (SPU) Center for Scholarship and Faculty Development from 2010 to 2016. In this role, I was responsible for various faculty
workshops in teaching and learning, the first-year faith and learning
seminar, educational technology, internal scholarship monies, sponsored
programs, faculty book clubs, and assigning mentors to new faculty. The
Center, now in its nineteenth year, had been founded by Susan VanZanten
in 2002 with a sizable grant from the Lilly Foundation. I'm grateful that
early- and midcareer faculty at SPU do not have to experience the terror
of just showing up and muddling on one's own through the long probationary period before tenure. I still remember that my overriding emotion
on learning that I had received tenure was relief.

Although traditional mentoring programs focus on building employee
competencies through a one-to-one relationship between a newcomer and
a seasoned employee, organizational socialization, such as we were attempting at SPU's Center, is a more complex multi-relational process that
is meant to facilitate a newcomer's adjustment not only to the new job but
to the workplace. Traditionally it has been "the process by which an individual acquires the attitudes, behavior, and knowledge needed to participate as an organizational member."[12] Intentional faculty socialization can
occur through work with a formally assigned mentor or informal insider,
peer support in and outside the institution, colleagues, one's chair, observation of the actions of significant others, exposure to the rituals and stories
the school tells about itself, and formal human resources (HR) programs,

---

[12]Andrea E. C. Griffin, Adrienne Colella, and Srikanth Goparaju, "Newcomer and Organizational
  Socialization Tactics: An Interactionist Perspective," *Human Resource Management Review* 10,
  no. 4 (2000): 453.

such as new-employee orientation and onboarding programs. Provosts, deans, department chairs, HR directors, Diversity, Equity and Inclusion (DEI) offices, directors of faculty development, and assigned mentors are coordinated to ensure that new faculty are part of a robust socialization process that includes institutional, cohort, and personalized opportunities to become competent, resilient, and fulfilled faculty members who see themselves living out their calling as valued organizational members.

Making the investment to socialize faculty beyond an initial orientation may seem like a luxury at a time when most institutions are faced with tight budgets that would not allow for one or more course releases or stipends for programming designed to assist new faculty with socialization. But the cost of not investing in socialization is significant. All employees start new jobs with uncertainty about their responsibilities and roles. Indeed, the "imposter syndrome," discussed later in this chapter, is a well-known psychological state where new employees are certain they will be fired once others catch on that they are not qualified and should not have been hired in the first place. Employees who receive little to no socialization have less clarity about their jobs, are less efficacious in carrying out their job responsibilities, feel less socially accepted, are less connected to a social network with its attendant access to information and other resources, are less satisfied with their jobs, are less committed, and are more likely to quit.[13] It should come as no surprise then that faculty who receive no socialization often withdraw from institutional life, too often burying themselves in their scholarship and a small cadre of colleagues and students. The free-agency mindset found in some older faculty can be a consequence of how they were treated early in their careers.

Given the negative consequences associated with poor organizational socialization, it isn't surprising that the topic is one of the oldest continuously studied areas in psychology, management, and organizational sciences. Over the past sixty years, three models of organizational socialization have emerged, each in response to the needs of its time and the

---

[13]Talya N. Bauer et al., "Newcomer Adjustment during Organizational Socialization: A Meta-Analytic Review of Antecedents, Outcomes, and Methods," *Journal of Applied Psychology* 92, no. 3 (2007): 707-21.

latter two building on the foundational work of the first. Even though most of the scholarship and practice of organizational socialization has not been framed within a theological understanding, the mutuality between individuals' calls and the responses from institutional missions shapes each approach to mentoring for organizational socialization. But which comes first? Each model, developed in the specific social location of its time, has a different emphasis on personal call or organizational mission. The early model started from a purely organizational focus. The second concerned newcomer adjustment. Then, in the past two decades, we see a move toward a more mutually reinforcing model.

THE INSTITUTIONAL MODEL

The earliest model was originally developed and researched in the 1960s by Edgar Schein, professor emeritus of work and organizational studies at the Sloan School of Management at MIT.[14] Professor Schein is recognized for his pioneering work in leadership and organizational culture, driving organizational change, and creating learning organizations. Known as the institutional model,[15] it is primarily designed to provide appropriate information to help employees "learn the ropes" of how to function in their new organization.[16] Socialization in this model is content heavy, taking a monolithic approach to newcomers in teaching them both to navigate effectively through their new workplaces and to adopt "the values, abilities, expected behaviors and social knowledge essential for participating as an organizational member."[17]

While this model was developed for a very different-looking workplace, it's still the primary way people think about socialization. And for good reason; there is much to appreciate in proactively helping employees to learn their jobs within the unique context of their organizations. Moving

[14]Edgar H. Schein, "Organizational Socialization and the Profession of Management," *Industrial Management Review* 9, no. 2 (1968): 1-16.
[15]Gareth R. Jones, "Socialization Tactics, Self-Efficacy, and Newcomers' Adjustments to Organizations," *Academy of Management Journal* 29, no. 2 (1986): 262-79.
[16]Alan M. Saks and Blake E. Ashforth, "Organizational Socialization: Making Sense of Past and Present as a Prologue for the Future," *Journal of Vocational Behavior* 51, no. 2 (1997): 236-37.
[17]Meryl Reis Louis, "Surprise and Sense Making: What Newcomers Experience in Entering Unfamiliar Organizational Settings," *Administrative Science Quarterly* 25, no. 2 (1980): 229-30.

away from the prevailing sink-or-swim model of newcomer adjustment, the legacy of this model is five functions that provide newcomers with relatively structured practices designed to introduce them to their organization.[18] Although this model has been used across multiple types of organizations and employees, it is quite suitable for orienting faculty through their early years in the professorate.

The first function is the design of the socialization process itself, ensuring a formal *structure* with regularly scheduled meetings and expected attendance. It needs to be *sequenced* in such a way as to meet the immediate needs of new faculty as their responsibilities unfold. It must be *spaced* to allow faculty to practice what is being asked of them. And it should be *cumulative* so that each time faculty are exposed to new expectations, it is linked to content with which they are already familiar, furthering adjustment in a sequential fashion. At the start, this can be a very focused orientation on what faculty need to be successful during their first week: professional development around course design and delivery, creating a syllabus, using classroom technology, legal issues in running a classroom, meeting their librarian liaisons, and meeting with the institution's counseling director to know what to do for a student in distress. Too often new faculty start with a two- or three-day data overload. As important as it will be in the future, do new faculty really need to meet with the director of the career center on their first week on the job?

The second function is a dedicated facilitator, such as the director of faculty development. This is the go-to person responsible for ensuring the correct flow of socialization experiences and appointing mentors who are not part of any formal evaluation of the new faculty member. Although such a facilitator may do the bulk of the training, their most important role is being the linking pin between new faculty and other aspects of the institution. This person has significant insider knowledge that can help with individualized socialization, answering questions or pointing new faculty to the correct person.

---

[18]Blake E. Ashforth, "The Role of Time in Socialization Dynamics," in *The Oxford Handbook of Socialization*, ed. Connie R. Wanberg (New York: Oxford University Press, 2012), 161-86.

The institutional model relies on a cohort, its third function, where new faculty go through the socialization process together. Although there is a "misery loves company" aspect to having new faculty spend significant time together their first year, it also ensures that new faculty have common learning experiences designed to produce standardized responses to situations. This group setting helps to reinforce expectations among new faculty, inculcating the common norms, values, and attitudes that are expected for institutional success. Over the years, faculty have regularly told me that their best friends outside of their department were members of their new-faculty cohort.

The fourth function ensures opportunities for new faculty to practice the craft of teaching outside of the classroom. Part of the socialization process should occur away from the evaluative "eyes" of chairs and more senior department members, providing faculty with a space of psychological safety where they can make mistakes and ask questions that they may believe would put them in a negative light of being incompetent. Many institutions have "learning labs," where faculty can practice teaching in front of invited peers, a few students, and / or the director of faculty development. Sessions can be taped so that those in attendance can provide feedback while watching it with the faculty member. In another example, after the first semester, it can be helpful for the person in charge of socialization to meet collectively with the new faculty cohort to work with them on how to read and make sense of their first set of course evaluations.

The final function is to frame the socialization process as part of an ongoing faculty development program. In this way, socialization does not have a fixed end but rather is a starting point for faculty that blends into more targeted development opportunities afforded to all faculty members.

While seemingly straight forward, this model takes a good deal of planning and coordination. Its cumulative approach recognizes that socialization requires new faculty's time and commitment to engage in the activities. A good socialization program provides a deep soak: opportunities to build relationships, learn, practice, get feedback, and improve in a caring community.[19] But the payoff is greater than faculty merely learning the ropes. The investment required by this welcoming approach signals care rather than indifference to new employees, and that alone has been shown to lower levels of ambiguity and conflict for newcomers, improve their job satisfaction, and increase the likelihood that they will stay.[20]

But, as noted above, the glaring gap in this model is that it does not address any unique aspects of the vocational calling of an institution's employees. It is all response without the call. Socialization is in one direction: getting new employees to feel comfortable in their new institution so they can be more efficient and effective in how the organization wants them to work.[21] Although learning the ropes is an important attribute of organizational socialization, Schein, and other researchers who followed, have gone on to show that there is organizational value in affirming and developing the identities and capabilities that employees bring to their new workplace.[22]

THE INTERACTIONIST MODEL

Starting in the 1990s, a more nuanced socialization model emerged, moving away from a sole focus on organizational expectations to understanding that newcomers have unique requirements and motivations. This interactionist model continues with the importance of socializing employees to the inner workings of their institutions, but it also recognizes that newcomers are motivated and proactive in their socialization and not merely empty vessels to be filled; they are actively trying to make sense of their new roles.[23] This model is still focused on the response side of the call, but it recognizes that individuals also bring individualized expectations, goals, and values. Whether it's the excitement of taking on a new professional role

[19]Paul Chelsen and Margaret Diddams, "A Caring Community," in *Campus Life: In Search of Community—Expanded Edition*, ed. Drew Moser and Todd C. Ream (Downers Grove, IL: IVP Academic, 2017), 52-60.

[20]Blake E. Ashforth and Alan M. Saks, "Socialization Tactics: Longitudinal Effects on Newcomer Adjustment," *Academy of Management Journal* 39, no. 1 (1996): 149-78.

[21]Sue Ashford and Samir Nurmohamed, "From Past to Present and into the Future: A Hitchhiker's Guide to the Socialization Literature," in *The Oxford Handbook of Socialization*, ed. Connie R. Wanberg (New York: Oxford University Press, 2012), 9.

[22]Bauer et al., "Newcomer Adjustment"; Van Maanen and Schein, "Toward a Theory of Organizational Socialization."

[23]Saks and Ashforth. "Organizational Socialization," 234-79.

or reducing the anxiety that goes with it, the interactionist model aims to enhance newcomers' adjustment to their organizations.

Although subtle, the shift is seismic; organizational socialization is no longer considered complete once new employees are run through orientation programs. Instead, socialization includes individualized processes designed to help newcomers adjust well to their work and enhance organizational identity, making the shift from "they" to "we."[24]

In addition, there is a greater understanding that newcomers, even those who have a strong sense of calling, are also entering into what the Franciscan priest and author Richard Rohr calls "deliberate displacement."[25] New employment always creates a liminal space, an uncertain present between the known past and the yet-knowable future, where people are leaving a place of competence to enter willingly into what amounts to a new world where, even if they are hired for their expertise, they are giving up the social knowledge of how to get things done, whom to turn to, and with whom to work. They have left a place of "business as usual" that gave the cognitive and emotional comfort of predictable, understandable, and ultimately controllable work to join an organization where they do not know the rules and expectations. Newcomers' sense of competency and identity takes a hit as they don't feel as efficacious as they did or think they should in this new setting.[26] It takes longer to get things done. (How do I work this copier?) It takes more mental energy to complete simple tasks. (How do I save my files on the server? Where did I save my files on the server?) The comfortable intuitive social system of the past is gone, and newcomers do not know what they do not know. Starting a new job is exciting but also exhausting; the gears of the new workplace have a grinding quality to them. In the interactionist model, the goal is to minimize the liminal space so newcomers' sense of calling more easily aligns with their organization's mission.

---

[24]Howard J. Klein, Beth Polin, and Kyra Leigh Sutton, "Specific Onboarding Practices for the Socialization of New Employees," *International Journal of Selection and Assessment* 23, no. 3 (2015): 263-83.

[25]Richard Rohr, *Adam's Return: The Five Promises of Male Initiation* (New York: Crossroad, 2004), 137.

[26]Louis, "Surprise and Sense Making," 230.

Recognizing this displacement, the interactionist model takes on a more individualized psycho-social approach. If the institutional model was focused on information and reducing organizational uncertainty through campus-wide programs, this model focuses on helping faculty adjust by reducing job uncertainties.[27] Learning the ins and outs of an institution is important for socialization, but robust research on the interactionist model indicates that individualized investment in newcomers holds significant value in employee well-being over and above what they will learn through the institutional model.[28]

Research on the interactionist model has consistently shown three important processes for newcomer adjustment: self-efficacy, role clarity, and social acceptance.[29] The first two are important for functioning well in the new job. The third addresses assimilation and identity.

Self-efficacy. Self-efficacy involves learning the job and gaining confidence at work without fear of failure. Although we all joke about having experienced the imposter syndrome sometime in our careers, it is no joke for those who are frozen by a foreboding sense of failure even before their first day of work. First identified in the late 1970s,[30] "imposter syndrome" describes the anxiety, often among intelligent and high-achieving people, of not being as capable or adequate as others appear to judge them to be. Those who suffer from it often see their past success as being based in luck and out of their control (e.g., they landed the right adviser as a doctoral student). They tend to have a fear of evaluation, a fear of not being able to repeat past successes, and a fear of being seen as less capable than they are.[31]

The misalignment between graduate training and the work expected of new faculty fuels this fear; they are not being prepared to take on the role of the

---

[27]Bauer et al., "Newcomer Adjustment."

[28]Blake E. Ashforth, David M. Sluss, and Alan M. Saks, "Socialization Tactics, Proactive Behavior, and Newcomer Learning: Integrating Socialization Models," *Journal of Vocational Behavior* 70, no. 3 (2007): 447-62.

[29]Bauer et al., "Newcomer Adjustment," 707; Daniel C. Feldman, "The Multiple Socialization of Organizational Members," *Academy of Management Review* 6, no. 1 (1981): 309-18.

[30]Pauline R. Clance and Susan A. Imes, "The Impostor Phenomenon in High Achieving Women: Dynamics and Therapeutic Intervention," *Psychotherapy: Theory, Research and Practice* 15, no. 3 (1978): 241-47.

[31]Sabine M. Chrisman et al., "Validation of the Clance Imposter Phenomenon Scale," *Journal of Personality Assessment* 65, no. 3 (1995): 456-67.

professorate. The emphasis for most newly minted PhDs has been on scholarship, theory development, grant writing, conducting original research, and having two or three significant publications before going on the job market. Yet even at the most prestigious research institutions, they will still need to teach, assess student outcomes, advise, be an overall team player, be called on by outsiders to comment as an expert in their fields, and eventually provide leadership through participation in shared governance. Perhaps for not a few, there is fear of the future when they know they will have to cut the cords to their doctoral advisers and make their own standing in the field.[32]

There is a real cost for new faculty who experience imposter syndrome. They are less likely to take risks and more likely to turn to perfectionism and overwork. All of this is underlined by anxiety and excessive worry, which takes a toll on health. Since new faculty members often do not know the job well enough to evaluate their own performance, their fears can be self-reinforcing.

To turn down the temperature on this anxiety, institutions need to recognize and acknowledge that this is a widespread phenomenon for new faculty. Organizational socialization in this case means moving away from the traditional evaluative model, where new faculty feel that they are on probation, to a developmental model that is heavy on feedback and light on judgment for a faculty member's first and perhaps even second year for those who are new to teaching. Rather than deans sitting in on a formal course evaluation, new faculty can be invited to observe senior faculty and discuss their own course philosophies and strategies. Faculty can be encouraged to experiment with new classes without fear of mistakes being held against them at a pretenure or tenure review.

Role clarity. Role clarity follows closely behind self-efficacy. Simply put, newcomers have role clarity when they understand what to do and how to function well in their new institutions. More importantly, newcomers have role clarity when they can put all the pieces of their new jobs together, knowing the priorities and appropriate time to allocate to different job responsibilities. Departmental chairs and deans can help with role clarity

---

[32]Joel Bothello and Thomas J. Roulet, "The Imposter Syndrome, or the Mis-Representation of Self in Academic Life," *Journal of Management Studies* 56, no. 4 (2019): 854–61.

by articulating expectations to navigate tenure successfully. All new faculty need encouragement to use their time well by not over-prepping courses or thinking that the only way to be a good citizen is to have an open door to students any time they are in the office. Creating checklists and milestones for new faculty can be extremely helpful in turning down the ambiguity inherent in an assistant professor appointment.

Social Acceptance. The third process is the social acceptance that comes with feeling liked and trusted by peers. Within the context of a well-developed socialization process, individual mentoring may matter most for social acceptance. An "insider" mentor who has a significant social network can help to kick-start a newcomer's social network to advance the sense of belongingness. A well-respected mentor can provide credibility through modeling collegiality with a newcomer, which reinforces the idea that the newcomer is "one of us."[33]

Another aspect of social acceptance is known as organizational identification—absorbing institutional norms and behavioral expectations. Newcomers experience social acceptance as they see their organizations as part of their own identities, as they move from *they* to *we*. As mentors and other insiders share their stories and model actions, newcomers come to understand the nuances of expectations—"how we do things around here." Without the peer support found in social acceptance, newcomers are likely to experience greater frustration and question whether they have made the right choice in accepting the new job.[34] Individual mentoring alongside organizational practices is a core component of the interactionist model, but it is not a substitute.[35] Individual mentoring should never be seen as a prophylactic and backfill for an organizational climate that does not address newcomer adjustment on a larger scale. New faculty gain more personal and professional benefits when they

---

[33]Ruolian Fang, Michelle K. Duffy, and Jason D. Shaw, "The Organizational Socialization Process: Review and Development of a Social Capital Model," *Journal of Management* 37, no. 1 (2011): 127-52.

[34]Bauer et al., "Newcomer Adjustment."

[35]Tammy D. Allen, Lillian T. Eby, Georgia T. Chao, and Talya N. Bauer, "Taking Stock of Two Relational Aspects of Organizational Life: Tracing the History and Shaping the Future of Socialization and Mentoring Research," *Journal of Applied Psychology* 102, no. 3 (2017): 324-37.

have mentors who have been trained to help them adjust within a larger framework of organizational socialization.[36]

The interactionist model is not a substitute for the institutional model; rather, it builds on the prior's formal practices while recognizing that each newcomer brings unique needs and motivations as they adjust to new jobs and organizations. Yet it is distinctly different in its goals. Success is shifted toward newcomer adjustment and not just initiation into organizational life, as found at the heart of the institutional model. Yet even the interactionist model falls short in preparing faculty for long-term, satisfying careers as it is still weighted toward institutional response, sometimes at the expense of individual calls. The final model recognizes both newcomers' needs and institutional expectations, creating a mutually reinforcing culture that honors organizational mission while promoting faculty personal and professional flourishing.

THE INCLUSION MODEL

In the first two models, the socialization process is commonly deemed successful when newcomers identify so well with their new organization that they reflect and promote its culture as part of their own identity. Socialization programs have been generally designed to help newcomers align their sense of personal call to their institutions' missions. But can strong organizational identification be too much of a good thing?[37] By the late 1970s John Van Maanen, who worked with Edgar Schein, recognized that a highly structured socialization process can dampen newcomer voice, identity, and innovation. There is a trade-off between developing strong and somewhat lockstep behavioral expectations to strengthen organizational mission and allowing newcomers to bring their talents to shape a more vibrant organization.[38] He referred to this as the tension

---

[36]Georgia T. Chao, "Mentoring and Organizational Socialization: Networks for Work Adjustment," in *The Handbook of Mentoring at Work: Theory, Research, and Practices*, ed. Belle Rose Ragins and Kathy E. Kram (Los Angeles: Sage Publications, 2007), 179-96.

[37]Daniel M. Cable, Francesca Gino, and Bradley R. Staats, "Breaking Them in or Eliciting Their Best? Reframing Socialization Around Newcomers' Authentic Self-Expression," *Administrative Science Quarterly* 58, no. 1 (2013): 1-36.

[38]Van Maanen and Shein, "Toward a Theory of Organizational Socialization."

between "divestiture," where people are expected to give up much of their personal identity to forge a strong group identity (such as Army recruits), and "investiture," where employees are encouraged to maintain their sense of self without having to become a different type of person or "pay their dues" before feeling accepted. None too surprisingly, employees who are more invested have greater job satisfaction and are less likely to think about quitting.[39]

Researchers over the past two decades have built on the idea of investiture, moving away from promoting employee organizational *identification* to advocating for policies where employees feel a greater sense of psychological *ownership* over their jobs and their organizations, creating opportunities for newcomers to shape their work environments.[40] In academia, where tenure is five to seven years down the road, the sense of not belonging, not feeling a sense of organizational ownership as a full-fledged member of the community, can be a grueling sense of probation where any public action, departmental meeting, or course evaluation may be a cause for concern.[41] Employees are likely to feel ownership when they have more positive interactions with their managers, less structured work environments, more autonomy, more say in decisions that affect them, and fewer expectations of having to earn the right to speak up (or out). Employees who have a sense of psychological ownership don't turn into free agents; they have more personal commitment to their institution and greater satisfaction with their work.[42]

The ideas of divestiture/investiture and organizational identity/ownership may have continued to be just another esoteric academic topic of inquiry. But the need to create flourishing workplaces for more diverse employees has become increasingly important over the past two

---

[39] Ashford, Sluss, and Saks, "Socialization Tactics."

[40] Jon L. Pierce, Tatiana Kostova, and Kurt T. Dirks, "Toward a Theory of Psychological Ownership in Organizations," *Academy of Management Review* 26, no. 2 (2001): 298-310.

[41] John Van Maanen, "Golden Passports: Managerial Socialization and Graduate Education," *Review of Higher Education* 6, no. 4 (1983): 435-55.

[42] Sarah Dawkins, Amy Wei Tian, Alexander Newman, and Angela Martin, "Psychological Ownership: A Review and Research Agenda," *Journal of Organizational Behavior* 38, no. 2 (2017): 163-83; Melissa G. Mayhew et al., "A Study of the Antecedents and Consequences of Psychological Ownership in Organizational Settings," *Journal of Social Psychology* 147, no. 5 (2007): 493.

decades. Robust research shows that merely increasing the proportion of female and racialized minorities in the workforce is not enough to attract and retain a modern workforce. With fewer young adults entering the workforce, organizations are realizing that hiring more diverse employees without changing existing policies and practices that engender disparate treatment could be problematic for institutional health.[43]

By 2005, managing diversity had expanded to include equity in organizational policies and inclusion where "people of all identities and many styles can be fully themselves while contributing to the larger collective, as valued and full members."[44] Corporations were beginning to examine their cultures, mores, values, policies, and expectations to ensure equitable treatment and feelings of belongingness.

Lynn Shore, professor of management at Colorado State University, has been a lead voice in managing inclusion in organizations. To explain inclusion, she and her colleagues created a two-by-two matrix with high and low valuing "belongingness" on the X axis and high and low valuing "uniqueness" on the Y axis. As seen in figure 3.1, employees judge inclusion based on how they perceive the value of their unique knowledge, skills, abilities, and other gifts and the extent to which they believe that they are welcomed members of their organizational community *apart from their work*. Those who perceive neither feel a sense of exclusion. Those who are valued for their work but with no sense of belongingness fall into the differentiation category; they can feel like "human-doings" rather than human beings. Assimilation occurs when employees feel that they must conform to what they see as the prevailing institutional ethos before being taken seriously. Only when employees feel valued for their work as well as their identity are they likely to feel a sense of value and inclusion as authentic institutional members.[45]

[43]Michàlle E. Mor Barak, "Inclusion Is the Key to Diversity Management, but What Is Inclusion?" *Human Service Organizations, Management, Leadership & Governance* 39, no. 2 (2015): 83-88.
[44]Bernardo M. Ferdman, "Paradoxes of Inclusion: Understanding and Managing the Tensions of Diversity and Multiculturalism," *Journal of Applied Behavioral Science* 53, no. 2 (2017): 235.
[45]Lynn M. Shore et al., "Inclusion and Diversity in Work Groups: A Review and Model for Future Research," *Journal of Management* 37, no. 4 (2011): 1262-89.

Figure 3.1. Inclusion framework

	Low Belongingness	High Belongingness
Low Value in Uniqueness	**Exclusion** Individual is not treated as an organizational insider with unique value in the work group, but there are other employees or groups who are insiders.	**Assimilation** Individual is treated as in insider in the work group when they conform to organizational/ dominant cultural norms and downplay uniqueness.
High Value in Uniqueness	**Differentiation** Individual is not treated as an organizational insider in the work group, but their unique character- istics are seen as valuable and required for group/organizational success.	**Inclusion** Individual is treated as an insider and also allowed/encouraged to retain uniqueness within the work group.

Source: Lynn M. Shore, Amy E. Randel, Beth G. Chung, et al., "Inclusion and Diversity in Work Groups: A Review and Model for Future Research," *Journal of Management* 37, no. 4 (2011): 1266. Reprinted by permission of SAGE Publications.

Although inclusion is usually framed within the goals of multiculturalism, its aspirations are laudable for all employees and are especially important for newcomers. Organizations foster inclusion when employees (1) believe that their ideas are taken into consideration and are involved in decisions that will affect them, (2) feel that they can be themselves at work and not worry that they will be under more scrutiny than others, and (3) have equal op- portunities to advance in their careers.[46] While exclusion can have negative effects on psychological well-being and even physical health, employees who experience the joint uniqueness and belongingness of inclusion show higher rates of creativity, more engagement with others, and are less likely to leave.[47]

Where the institutional model ignores individual giftings and the inter- actionist model focuses on facilitating the adjustment of newcomers to reduce the stress of uncertainty, the inclusion model of socialization seeks to support faculty flourishing from the moment they become aware of the job opening. In turn, institutions use new-faculty socialization as an op- portunity to question existing cultural norms and practices that could

---

[46]Griffin Moores, "Inclusion in the Workplace: What It Means and Why Business Should Care," *Colorado State University College of Business Source*, November 14, 2017, https://biz.source.colo state.edu/inclusion-workplace-means-business-care/.

[47]Lynn M. Shore, Jeanette N. Cleveland, and Diana Sanchez, "Inclusive Workplaces: A Review and Model," *Human Resource Management Review* 28, no. 2 (2018): 176-89.

hinder that flourishing. They anticipate that changes for new faculty would positively affect all employees.

This model is a true call and response, where newcomers and their institutions each advance the flourishing of the other. As the person most responsible for new faculty orientation during my time as an SPU administrator, I quickly realized that I was also a safe place for them to admit what wasn't working for them, whether it was schedules, classrooms, offices, or interactions with students. To do my job well, I was not only directly responsible for faculty development, but I also served as a linking pin to academic administration and HR, advocating for changes in policies and procedures so that new faculty could thrive and move into more senior ranks without the bitterness and withdrawal that can occur when new hires are left to thrash about on their own. While I didn't then label my work in terms of an inclusion mode, in advocating for new faculty in other areas of the institution, I was improving equity and inclusion for many more.

Newcomers can be like the small boy in "The Emperor's New Clothes": when experiencing novelties, surprises, and contrasts with their expectations or previous experiences, they wind up shining a new light on old ways of working that insiders no longer question.[48] In the inclusion model, newcomers are encouraged to be interlocutors, to shape the culture and to contribute to the understanding of how their organizational mission is enacted.

Hiring new faculty is a perfect example of how the inclusion model can work. Although organizations have written policies, defined goals, cultivated values, and articulated aspirations about themselves, the method by which candidates are ranked and chosen help reveal the alignment between an institution's espoused values and how they are practiced.[49] Are candidates ranked highly based on their teaching experience, or does their program of research garner greater excitement? Is evidence of collaboration and collegiality valued? How important are past training and scholarship related to Bible and theology in candidate rankings?

---

[48]Louis, "Surprise and Sense Making," 237-39.
[49]Robert Simons, *Levers of Control: How Managers Use Innovative Control Systems to Drive Strategic Renewal* (Boston: Harvard Business Review Press, 1995), 33-57.

Under this model, hiring is part of the socialization process, and institutions interrogate each step starting with the job posting itself.[50] Its wording and emphases begin to signal to applicants what they can expect from the organization. Is it worded in a welcoming way, or is it a challenge to potential employees to question their worthiness to apply? Are job candidates told that it will be a highly selective process, which is likely to amp up the imposter syndrome? Are encouragements for diverse candidates boilerplates, or do they appear sincere? What materials must candidates submit? If there are essays or letters of inquiry, what must the candidate include and what is left out? How quickly does the institution reply after receiving the application materials? Do search committee members receive training on how to avoid bias in evaluating candidates? The interviews as well as the people involved in the interviewing are also part of the socialization process, setting expectations for newcomers of how to interact with administrative structures and the type of relationships that they are likely to have with their future coworkers.[51]

Unfortunately, institutions of higher education often treat campus interviews as a multiday gauntlet with successful candidates able to weather obtuse questions, with too much weight being placed on isolated incidents during the interview process. Under the inclusion model, the hiring process is designed to align with the institution's stated mission. To the extent that the process is out of step with espoused values, academic administrators take a deep look at inclusion policies to ensure newcomers can start their jobs having already developed a sense of belonging, fairness, and trust.

Furthermore, any adjustments are likely to benefit all employees. This interlocutor process becomes important for all status decisions. Are institutions acting out of their values and fairness when it comes to pretenure evaluations, tenure, promotion, and other faculty assignments? Are there opportunities for faculty to receive positive feedback and affirmation on a regular basis, or do they hear only secondhand complaints? How are

---

[50]This is also known as anticipatory socialization. See Jon C. Carr, et al., "Prior Occupational Experience, Anticipatory Socialization, and Employee Retention," *Journal of Management* 32, no. 3 (2006): 343–59.

[51]H. Jack Walker et al., "Is This How I Will Be Treated? Reducing Uncertainty Through Recruitment Interactions," *Academy of Management Journal* 56, no. 5 (2013): 1325-47.

student feedback forms used for developmental purposes and evaluations? What kinds of community are available for new faculty? Is there a cohort with whom they can build relationships, and are such communities available for all faculty in and outside of their departments? Returning full circle to mission statements like Baylor's, integrating academic excellence and Christian commitment takes the type of caring community found in the inclusion model.

CONCLUSION

In the past two decades, there have been more than two hundred academic articles on calling at work. It should come as no surprise that employees with a strong sense of calling are more involved at work when they perceive that their workplace values their contribution, gives them autonomy to do their work as they see fit, and cares about their well-being.[52] Intentional organizational socialization recognizes that an individual call is a call into community with the goal that all employees will be able to feel supported, included, valued, and productive.

Mentoring is not just the work of mentors. In a caring community, everyone is responsible for the privilege and burden of ensuring the flourishing of one another. An institution's mission is never merely outward focused; it always includes, whether espoused or merely practiced, some impact, for better or worse, on the welfare of its employees. Institutions ignore the internal effects at their peril. Organizational research clearly shows that there are significant benefits for both employees and their institutions when newcomers are formally and collectively socialized in a fixed, specified sequence.[53]

All three models provide important aspects for launching new faculty successfully. The institutional model reminds us that mentoring must be intentional. Many, including the provost, deans, chairs, HR, DEI

---

[52]Jiyoung Park et al., "Having a Calling on Board: Effects of Calling on Job Satisfaction and Job Performance Among South Korean Newcomers," *Frontiers in Psychology* 10 (2019): 1584; Ryan D. Duffy et al., "Examining the Effects of Contextual Variables on Living a Calling over Time," *Journal of Vocational Behavior* 107 (2018): 141-52.

[53]Alan M. Saks, Krista L. Uggerslev, and Neil E. Fassina, "Socialization Tactics and Newcomer Adjustment: A Meta-Analytic Review and Test of a Model," *Journal of Vocational Behavior* 70, no. 3 (2007): 413-16.

administrators, faculty development liaison, and assigned mentors, share responsibility for faculty socialization. It reminds us that mentoring is not merely interpersonal, but also structural and sequential. Mentoring a cohort of new faculty together starts to build a web of relationships that is likely to hold for years after the first newcomer orientation. Finally, the institutional model reminds us that mentoring is an important organizational process across the tenure of employees. New chairs and deans also require intentional organizational support.

The interactionist model reminds us that starting a new job is akin to going to a new country with only a rudimentary understanding of the language; it is full of shock and surprises.[54] All newcomers face significant adjustments, and the imposter syndrome often lurks just out of the sight of others. It reminds us that not all mentoring relationships are likely to be successful, with those who have insider knowledge of people and processes making for better mentors. Other employees, regardless of their designation as a mentor, model expectations while their stories provide insight into how "things get done around here." Most important, the interactionist model reminds us that socialization isn't so much about the organization as it is about newcomers. The interactionist model reminds us of the importance of taking a developmental rather than probationary approach to pretenured faculty, allowing for risk and failure. Finally, it reminds us that successful socialization doesn't conclude at the end of formal programing. Instead, socialization is successful when newcomers have increased their self-efficacy, role clarity, and social acceptance.

The inclusion model reminds us that new faculty are most likely to flourish when they are welcomed from the beginning as important members rather than perceiving that in order to be accepted they must modify how they "show up."[55] The model recognizes that newcomers can influence constructive change and innovation.[56] Institutions benefit when

---

[54]Louis, "Surprise and Sense Making," 244.

[55]Louis, "Surprise and Sense Making," 443.

[56]Blake E. Ashforth, David M. Sluss, and Spencer H. Harrison, "Socialization in Organizational Contexts," in *International Review of Industrial and Organizational Psychology*, ed. Gerald P. Hodgkinson and J. Kevin Ford (Hoboken, NJ: J. Wiley, 2007), 26.

employees believe they are trusted community members whose knowledge and skills are respected. Newcomer belongingness and uniqueness advocated by the inclusion model are crucial for *all faculty* to flourish. The inclusion model reminds us that organizational socialization is an opportunity to ensure alignment between espoused and enacted values, strengthening organizational mission.

Organizational socialization is not merely an investment in new faculty; it is also an investment in institutional mission. The call of God on the lives of faculty is a precious gift deserving a purposely shaped supportive response from a caring community. In return, the missions of colleges and universities become both more focused and expansive. When done well, there is a true "call and response" between faculty and their institutions. Organizational socialization matters.

4

DIVERSITY AND COMMUNITY

Mentoring Toward a New We

EDGARDO COLÓN-EMERIC

For more than a decade, I have had the privilege of supporting the training of pastors for Methodist churches in Central America. Twice a year, students from Honduras, Nicaragua, Guatemala, and El Salvador gather in Ahuachapán, a town near the border of El Salvador and Guatemala, for a week of intensive studies. It is a culturally and generationally diverse community of women and men, *mestizos* and Indigenous, Spanish speakers and Kiché speakers. The diversity of these Central American communities meets the diversity of the instructional team, which includes faculty connected to Duke University Divinity School and regional schools. During the week of classes, this diversity of peoples becomes a theological community sharing lessons, meals, worship, and the occasional spontaneous soccer match. It is a veritable seminary on wheels as the school goes on the road from Ahuachapán to various destinations around San Salvador for contextual learning experiences. The bus is our most common mode of transport and serves as a rolling classroom where people study, sing, and share stories on the way to our next destination. The buses are typically decommissioned yellow public school buses from the United States, but, in our journeys, they become divinity bus schools where a new *we* is cultivated for the sake of the church's mission in the world.

I begin with this story because I believe the experience of theological education in Central America and the dreams from the American Global South belong to the context for which we mentor Millennials in North

America. Much conversation around mentoring is methodological: How do we mentor new generations of scholars? The question I would like to explore is teleological: Mentoring toward what end? I propose we are mentoring toward a new *we* that, like the Central American bus school, is formed on the road.

The chapter begins with a brief overview of the context in which mentoring happens. The theological academy, for example, is becoming more ethnically diverse. At the same time, historically underrepresented people continue to face challenges to their belonging, exposing the limitations of the current social location and design of the theological academy. After this diagnostic survey, I consider the work of the Center for Reconciliation in the American Global South as one way of mentoring dreamers of a more just, inclusive *we* for the North American academy in its Pentecost journey.

AN INCREASINGLY DIVERSE ACADEMIC LANDSCAPE

Generational diversity is not new. Aristotle describes young people: "Changeable in their desires and soon tiring of them, they desire with extreme ardor, but soon cool; for their will, like the hunger and thirst of the sick, is keen rather than strong."[1] Clearly, Aristotle intends to name perennial characteristics of the young, a permanent generational gap. Aristotle's modern counterparts engage this gap through a generational analysis that oversimplifies and abstracts in order to describe the main traits of today's generations. Millennials, we are often told, are more racially diverse, less religious, more socially conscious, less career oriented, and so forth.[2] Generalizations abound, yet the task of understanding generational differences is most productive when undertaken with humility.

---

[1]Aristotle, *The Art of Rhetoric* 2.12, ed. and trans. John Henry Freese (London: W. Heinemann, 1926). See the Perseus Digital Library, www.perseus.tufts.edu/hopper/text?doc=Perseus%3Atext%3A1999.01.0060%3Abook%3D2%3Achapter%3D12.

[2]For example, Millennial desires for social awareness and a work-life balance feature in Claire Cain Miller and Sanam Yar, "Young People Are Going to Save Us All from Office Life," *New York Times*, September 17, 2019, www.nytimes.com/2019/09/17/style/generation-z-millennials-work-life-balance.html.

As Paul Taylor states, "All of us know people who bear the marks of their distinctive coming-of-age experiences: the grandmother raised during the Depression who still reuses her tea bags; the uncle who grew up in the 1960s and still sports a ponytail; the kid sister who sends 200 texts a day to her many, many best friends."[3] As the preceding examples illustrate, generational analysis can carry the implicit biases of the social location of the analyst. In *Citizens but Not Americans*, Nilda Flores-González studies how Latinx Millennials in the Chicago area define themselves in ways that disrupt the White-Black paradigm that dominates US discourses of belonging.[4] These young people understand themselves "as an ethnorace, a racial middle, and 'real' Americans."[5] I mention this not simply to make the banal point that no generation is monolithic but the more important point that the literature on Millennials and the church has not always sufficiently attended to the racial and ethnic makeup of these generations.[6]

Ethnic diversity is not new. Imperial capitals like Rome were multicultural centers of commerce. Even Jerusalem—a colonized, marginal city—experienced and struggled with diversity (as seen in Acts 2). What is new is how diversity is interpreted and experienced. The ancient systems of organizing diversity hierarchically (men over women, old over young, citizen over slave, Roman over barbarian, the West over the rest, and so forth) no longer light the way, even if they still cast a long shadow. Gustavo Gutiérrez named the irruption of the poor as one of the most important signs of the twentieth century. Not that the poor were ever absent; rather,

---

[3]Paul Taylor, *The Next America: Boomers, Millennials, and the Looming Generational Showdown* (New York: PublicAffairs, 2014), 32.

[4]Nilda Flores-González, *Citizens but Not Americans: Race and Belonging Among Latino Millennials* (New York: New York University Press, 2017).

[5]Flores-González, *Citizens but Not Americans*, 151. For these Millennials, the generational and the ethnoracial are intrinsically intertwined: "Ancestry, skin color and phenotype, social class, education, gender, language, and aspects of culture converged and shape how these youths experience and navigate everyday racialization" (7).

[6]David Kinnaman's *You Lost Me* speaks powerfully to the challenges facing congregations in retaining their youth. The book has been the subject of study guides and has even been translated to Spanish. See Kinnaman, *You Lost Me: Why Young Christians Are Leaving Church . . . and Rethinking Faith* (Grand Rapids, MI: Baker Books, 2011). Nevertheless, the struggles of Latinx Millennials as narrated by Flores-González lie beyond the scope of that classic work, and the book resonated little with my experience as a pastor of a Latinx congregation where the younger generation literally had a different sense of belonging to the US context than their parents who spoke Spanish and were undocumented.

before the twentieth century, the poor were seen as extras rather than actors in history, as subjects rather than agents.

Willie James Jennings sees a parallel phenomenon unfolding in the theological academy: "The invasion of predominately White theological institutions by racial and ethnic minorities is one of the single most important changes in theological education in the latter half of the twentieth century and the beginning of the twenty-first century."[7] Jennings's use of the term *invasion* is provocative and points to perceptions common among members of the dominant community. The reality is quite different. According to data collected by the Association of Theological Schools, in the year 2000, there were ninety-one Hispanic faculty among a total of 3,299 full-time faculty. In 2020, the number grew to 142 out of 2,879—meaning 4.9 percent of full-time faculty is Hispanic.[8] Meanwhile, 18.5 percent of the US population is Hispanic.[9] The diversification of the academy is more of an expeditionary foray than a full-fledged invasion.

Schools have long experience with generational diversity. The annual turnover of students and the regular cycles of faculty and staff rotations require schools to rearticulate and renew the ethos of the community. On the other hand, schools are less experienced in welcoming racial and ethnic diversity in ways that foster belonging—and this is because of the design and condition of the roads to theological education.

THE ROADS TO THEOLOGICAL EDUCATION

Theological pluralism and theological education are correlates. A diversity of schools follows from the variety of ways in which the task of understanding God is construed and manifested. David Kelsey describes

[7]Willie James Jennings, "The Change We Need: Race and Ethnicity in Theological Education," *Theological Education* 49, no. 1 (2015): 35.

[8]The Association of Theological Schools online resources, www.ats.edu/uploads/resources/institutional-data/annual-data-tables/2004-2005-annual-data-tables.pdf and www.ats.edu/files/galleries/2019-2020_Annual_Data_Tables.pdf.

[9]Latinx theologian-ethicists make a similar observation in Rubén Rosario Rodríguez et al., "US Latino/a Contributions to the Field: Retrospect and Prospect," *Journal of the Society of Christian Ethics* 38, no. 2 (Fall 2018): 45-56, at 46. For census data, see "B03002 Hispanic or Latino Origin by Race, United States, 2019 American Community Survey 1-Year Estimates," United States Census Bureau (July 1, 2019), https://data.census.gov/cedsci/table?q=B03002&g=0100000US&tid=ACSDT1Y2019.B03002&hidePreview=true.

the Christian theological school as a village built at the crossroads of Berlin and Athens. By this metaphor, Kelsey locates theological education as the result of a conversation between the Enlightenment approach to knowledge as science (*Wissenschaft*, of which the University of Berlin is emblematic) and the Greco-Roman emphasis on character formation (*paideia*, here associated with Athens). Kelsey adds an ecclesial connector between these two roads, which gives the theological school doctrinal and historic specificity:

> Theological schools are academic hamlets located at crossroads, one of which is the road from (select at least one): Nicaea, Trent, Augsburg, Geneva, Canterbury, Northampton, Asuza Street Mission, and so forth. Each of those place names is the emblem of a different way of construing the *subject matter* on which a theological school focuses.[10]

Mentoring implies induction into the way in which a particular school sits at the crossroads. My own Duke University Divinity School is a theological village found at the intersection of Berlin, Athens, and Aldersgate.[11] However, as Fred Herzog (a former Duke professor) observed, Kelsey's map is clearly a Northern-Hemisphere projection.[12] Orienting theological education around Berlin (science), Athens (formation), and Aldersgate (tradition) keeps poverty off the map. Herzog writes, "In a strange way, our theological schools in the North often have been able to seal themselves off from their mission to all non-persons existing on the margins of our cities and our country."[13] Expanding the map to include Lima, as Herzog suggests, presents the possibility of learning from the theological creativity, curiosity, and capacity of scholarly voices not frequently heard in the Global North. Even when the map is redrawn and reoriented to include local and global peripheries, there remains the challenge of access.

---

[10]David Kelsey, *To Understand God Truly: What's Theological About a Theological School* (Louisville, KY: Westminster John Knox, 1992), 32.

[11]See my article on this subject, Edgardo Colón-Emeric, "Maintaining Good Roads: The Relationship Between Duke Divinity School and Methodism," *Divinity* (Spring 2014): 59. "Aldersgate" refers to a key historical site and moment of Methodism's origins and here names Duke Divinity School's ties to the Methodist tradition.

[12]Frederick Herzog, "Athens, Berlin, and Lima," *Theology Today* 51, no. 2 (1994): 270-76.

[13]Herzog, "Athens, Berlin, and Lima," 273.

The roads connecting Berlin, Athens, and Aldersgate are better maintained than the roads connecting these to Lima, Ahuachapán, or even east Durham (which lies on the other side of the railroad tracks from Duke). Moreover, people coming from communities that are historically underrepresented in theological education must pay an extra toll for traveling these roads. Patrick Reyes speaks eloquently to this problem in *The Purpose Gap*:

> Cultural commutes are some of the greatest barriers to closing the purpose gap, and we are not just talking about a few extra minutes in traffic on the freeway or bus. Not only do the oppressed have to overcome historic injustices, but we must also contend with modern designs built on those histories. If we want future generations to thrive, many of us are traveling extremely far to the sources of power. The cultural commute is more than just the physical miles from Brown neighborhoods to white concentrations of power; it also includes the cultural travel: the code switching, translating, and learning to survive a game that is designed for us to lose.[14]

Everything from the social location of the theological academy to its curricular architectural design to its co-curricular furnishings conspire to tell nonwhite scholars that they are, at best, guests. Willie Jennings observes that "the blood of the theological academy has changed thanks to the presence of minorities, but this new blood does not yet circulate with ease through the body."[15] Indeed, their presence may be experienced as a foreign element and stimulate an immune response. Andrea Smith has argued that the university needs to be understood "as an ideological state apparatus designed to reify the settler colonialist, white supremacist and capitalist status quo."[16]

Black and Brown faculty who have survived this theological commute can mentor others and give advice to make the commute bearable. They can play a role similar to the phone map applications that warn drivers of slowdowns and accidents and offer alternative routes that save time. But

---

[14]Patrick B. Reyes, *The Purpose Gap: Empowering Communities of Color to Find Meaning and Thrive* (Louisville, KY: Westminster John Knox, 2021), 51.

[15]Jennings, "The Change We Need," 36.

[16]Andrea Smith, "Life After Tenure Denial," in *Mentoring Faculty of Color: Essays on Professional Development and Advancement in Colleges and Universities*, ed. Dwayne Mack, Elwood D. Watson, and Michelle Madsen Camacho (Jefferson, NC: McFarland, 2013), 197.

closing the purpose gap calls for mentors who are more than Google Maps. As Reyes explains, "If society was designed to marginalize and oppress us, closing the purpose gap means creating alternative worlds where the cultural commute does not exist, where people can live and thrive on their own terms and see themselves reflected in the design."[17]

One way to achieve this goal is by retreating into a cultural cul-de-sac or a gated community that promotes and protects the internal identity from external exchanges. Willie Jennings acknowledges that "a number of scholars of color carry an abiding skepticism that Christian intellectual formation can be anything other than white European masculinist formation. That skepticism, founded at the opening moments of colonial conquest, yet grows and fosters a quiet despair that moves through the educational ecologies of theological schools."[18] The way forward that Jennings proposes is the decolonial path: "Theological education in the Western world has entered a new stage where it must develop authentically decolonial habits of mind that transform theological schools into places that educate people toward one another and not simply beside one another."[19]

Now, as Michael Ignatieff argues, the ordinary virtues that facilitate living side by side in a chaotic world are not to be breezily dismissed.[20] Maintaining collegial relations among faculty who are diverse in many ways (racially, generationally, theologically, and so forth) and are pursuing research in different academic disciplines is a rare achievement in today's polarized world. Nevertheless, more than collegiality is pressing and possible because theological education happens after Pentecost—a theme to which I will return at the end of the chapter.

It is not possible to address matters of mentoring underrepresented minority faculty without considering stories of pain and exclusion.

---

[17]Reyes, *Purpose Gap*, 51.

[18]Willie James Jennings, *After Whiteness: An Education in Belonging* (Grand Rapids, MI: Eerdmans, 2020), 14.

[19]Jennings, "The Change We Need," 42.

[20]Michael Ignatieff, *The Ordinary Virtues: Moral Order in a Divided World* (Cambridge, MA: Harvard University Press, 2017). Ignatieff states, "Living side by side, as opposed to living together, does not require much meeting of minds or even shared culture. It requires passably fair public institutions, decent policing above all and a subliminal operating system—basic trust, basic reciprocity—constantly tested, constantly renegotiated, but usually reaffirmed in the ebb and flow of daily life" (45).

However, it would be a mistake to portray the journey of minority scholars in predominantly white institutions as an unrelenting via dolorosa. It is more like a pilgrimage of pain and hope toward a new *we*.

MESTIZAJE: A PILGRIMAGE OF PAIN AND HOPE

The future roads of theological education go through *mestizaje*. The end is not a compartmentalized diversity with each people group in its own silo but a genuine togetherness that does not force assimilation to any one paradigm of formation, however venerable.[21] Hispanic/Latinx theologians turn to the concept of *mestizaje* to name the movement toward a new *we*. As Néstor Medina explains, "The initial adoption of *mestizaje* by U.S. Latina/o theologians was a move away from ethnocentric views. As they saw it, they could no longer emphasize one culture as a finished product but instead focused on the ancestral cultural strands that contributed to the formation of the Latina/o cultural expressions."[22]

The usage of *mestizaje* in Latinx theology is complex and not without its critics.[23] As Rubén Rosario Rodríguez notes, decolonial thinkers worry that it "perpetuates the modern/colonial world system by creating the idea of a homogeneous Latin American *mestizo* identity as 'other' to the colonial power without fully recognizing the cultural heterogeneity of Latin America."[24] The concern is well founded in the Latin American experience.[25] A communal identity built on a mestizo cosmic race would replay

---

[21]See Willie James Jennings, "Race and the Educated Imagination: Outlining a Pedagogy of Belonging," *Religious Education* 112, no. 1 (2016): 63.

[22]Néstor Medina, *Mestizaje: (Re)Mapping Race, Culture, and Faith in Latina/o Catholicism* (Maryknoll, NY: Orbis, 2009), 12.

[23]For a thorough overview of *mestizaje* especially in Latinx theology, see Néstor Medina, "U.S. Latina/o Theology: Challenges, Possibilities, and Future Prospects," in *Theology and the Crisis of Engagement*, ed. Jeff Nowers and Néstor Medina (Eugene, OR: Pickwick, 2013), 141-60. See also Medina's entry "Mestizaje" in *Encyclopedia of Christianity in the Global South*, ed. Mark A. Lamport (Lanham, MD: Rowman & Littlefield, 2018), 500-502. For Virgilio Elizondo's original articulation, see his *Galilean Journey: The Mexican-American Promise* (Maryknoll, NY: Orbis, 2006). See also Rubén Rosario Rodríguez, *Racism and God-Talk: A Latino/a Perspective* (New York: New York University Press, 2008).

[24]Rubén Rosario Rodríguez, *Racism and God-Talk*, 73.

[25]The Spanish encouraged *mestizaje* as a tool of conquest. Two things followed from the marriage of Spanish soldiers to Indigenous princesses. On the one hand, the perceived impurity of the Indigenous hues and habits would be cleansed. On the other hand, the Spanish would become caciques and rightly rule the Indigenous. (See Suzanne Bost, *Mulattas and Mestizas: Representing*

the experiences of the independence movements in Latin America, where mestizo was oriented toward whiteness and away from peoples of African and Indigenous descent.[26] In this regard, *mestizaje* is to be preferred to mestizo because the former draws attention to the process of mixing and away from a finished product, a more perfect *tertium quid*.

Rosario Rodríguez speaks of *mestizaje* as a theological metaphor and transcultural paradigm that bears witness to the painful history of conquest, enslavement, and cultural and ethnic genocide of the Americas in order to work for its liberation and transformation. *Mestizaje*, then, entails "a new way of being in relationship with one another."[27] A community formed through *mestizaje* is a sign that "the painful history of being both the oppressed and the oppressor" can be healed.[28] In this way, *mestizaje* is indeed a pilgrimage of pain and hope toward a new *we* that is more just and mysterious because it is both christological and eschatological. In the words of 1 John 3:2, "What we will be has not yet been revealed. What we do know is this: when he is revealed, we will be like him, for we will see him as he is" (NRSV).

The Center for Reconciliation at Duke University Divinity School seeks to mentor pilgrims for this mysterious *mestizaje*. By engaging in a common journey of theological, prayerful, embodied reflection *en conjunto* (together) with fellow Christian scholars and practitioners from diverse racial

---

Mixed Identities in the Americas, 1850–2000 [Athens: University of Georgia Press, 2005], 27-30.) Indeed, in the 1850s, two priests devised a plan for national Mexican unity, the basis of which lay in convening a congress of the twelve closest relatives of Montezuma to elect an emperor. This man, if White, would marry an Indigenous woman; if Indigenous, a White one. See Marilyn Grace Miller, *Rise and Fall of the Cosmic Race: The Cult of Mestizaje in Latin America* (Austin: University of Texas Press, 2004), 28.

[26]The national identity of the new republics was built by privileging whiteness and eurocentrism to the detriment of other identities. The Black and Indigenous elements of the culture were romanticized and historicized for the sake of a *mestizo* (not Indian or Black) identity. Simón Bolivar is a case in point. He presented *mestizaje* as both a sign of and a means to the formation of an American identity independent from Spain. Racial and ethnic difference was minimized and leveled for the sake of unity in the cause of sovereign independence. For instance, he offered manumission to slaves who took up arms against Spain. Nevertheless, despite appreciating and calling for *mestizaje* in the struggle, Bolivar viewed the component elements of *mestizaje* in stereotypical ways. In his vision of the national future, the Whites would be the brains, the Brown the land, and the Blacks the brawn. See Miller, *Rise and Fall of the Cosmic Race*, 8-11.

[27]Rosario Rodríguez, *Racism and God-Talk*, 100.

[28]Rosario Rodríguez, *Racism and God-Talk*, 109.

and ethnic backgrounds, we nurture a sense of belonging to God's movement for radical reconciliation. Our *we* is reviewed, renewed, and reformed through practices such as social dislocation, solidarity with Christian witnesses from the peripheries, and sustained examination of questions such as these: (1) Where are we going? Reconciliation toward what? (2) What is going on? And how did we get here? (3) What does hope look like? What are the stories that interrupt us? (4) Why me? And why bother? Each day is accompanied by naming gifts (new creation, lament, liberation, and vocation) given by God to empower the expansion of a just and reconciling *we* that reaches out to all peoples (not only Christians) and all creatures (not only human).[29] Pope Francis's Encyclical Letter *Fratelli tutti* presents the vision of this new *we* with gospel simplicity:

> No one can face life in isolation. . . . We need a community that supports and helps us, in which we can help one another to keep looking ahead. How important it is to dream together. . . . By ourselves, we risk seeing mirages, things that are not there. Dreams, on the other hand, are built together.[30]

Dreams are built together. Mentoring pilgrims for an honest and hopeful *mestizaje* in the theological academy calls for mentoring dreamers of a new *we*. This new *we* rejects living apart and responding to difference with fear and fearmongering. The new *we* dreams of more than living side by side. The ordinary virtues of tolerance and civility are valuable and even necessary, but they are only a step on the way. "Coexist" may be a good bumper sticker for navigating the complex cloverleaf exchanges of theological education, but it is a bleak billboard for the destination. A new *we* dreams of living together.[31]

---

[29] As Jennings puts it, "What we need is a vision of education that aims at cultivating deep structures of belonging. . . . I envision this activity of faith to be inclusive and open for peoples of other faiths as well." "Race and the Educated Imagination," 63.

[30] Pope Francis, *Fratelli tutti*, encyclical letter (October 3, 2021), sec. 8, see the Vatican website www .vatican.va/content/francesco/en/encyclicals/documents/papa-francesco_20201003_enciclica -fratelli-tutti.html.

[31] There are parallels here with what Andrew Walls calls the Ephesian moment. See Andrew Walls, *The Cross-Cultural Process in Christian History* (Maryknoll, NY: Orbis, 2002). In the all-too-brief season in Ephesus, when Jews and Gentiles joined in intimate Christian community, a new way of being human was signified. From this Ephesian moment, Walls asks a question: "The Ephesian question at the Ephesian moment is whether or not the church in all its diversity will demonstrate its unity by the interactive participation of all its culture-specific segments, the interactive

DREAMS FROM THE AMERICAN GLOBAL SOUTH

These are the dreams we are dreaming in the Americas Initiative for Transformation and Reconciliation. The Center for Reconciliation has partnered with God and other Christian institutions in midwifing four initiatives for reconciliation. Each initiative has Indigenous leadership and ecumenical membership committed to sharing the gospel of reconciliation within their native lands.[32] They share a common vision: Jesus Christ is the Word made flesh, through whom God seeks to reconcile all things. This vision is theological and necessarily contextual precisely because *becoming flesh* means becoming culture, becoming history, becoming people, becoming community. This vision guides and orients the daily lives of people on a common journey of painful and hopeful *mestizaje*. In the case of the Americas Initiative, in addition to churches, universities, and seminaries, we also receive support from Christian NGOs such as the Programa Latinoamericano de Tierras, which addresses the persistent challenges around land ownership and use in Latin America; Memoria Indígena, which empowers Indigenous churches to recognize and be recognized for their Indigenous identity; and Peace and Hope International, which addresses issues of environmental justice, peace building and violence prevention. This list names not only some of our partners but some of the wounds in the Latin American and diaspora contexts in desperate need of healing.

What are we learning from the American Global South that might inform and inspire our dreams of a new *we*? Note, this initiative just celebrated its one-year anniversary in the autumn of 2021. It is very

---

participation that is to be expected in a functioning body" (81). Walls also raises a still-valid warning: "There are two dangers. One lies in an instinctive desire to protect our own version of Christian faith, or even to seek to establish it as the standard normative one. The other, and perhaps the more seductive in the present condition of Western Christianity, is the postmodern option: to decide that each of the expressions and versions is equally valid and authentic, and that we are therefore each at liberty to enjoy our own in isolation from all the others" (78-79).

[32]The initiatives in chronological order: (1) The Great Lakes Institute gathers Christians from churches and nonprofits in East Africa. (2) The Summer Institute for Reconciliation gathers scholars, students and practitioners from Duke, North Carolina, and the United States. (3) The Northeast Asia Reconciliation Initiative brings together Christians from Japan, Korea, China, Taiwan, and Hong Kong. (4) The Americas Initiative for Transformation and Reconciliation includes people from Latin America and the Hispanic/Latinx diaspora in the United States.

much in its infancy. Our partnerships are not yet fully formed, and we are still seeking to include more Catholic institutions and more Afro-Latino perspectives. However, our first year of encounters gathered scholars and practitioners with decades of service.[33] For now, let me offer a few preliminary lessons.

First, the American Global South groans for a new *we*. Many feel a restlessness with the status quo. The slogan "another world is possible" resonates, especially with the youth. At the same time, this restlessness must be transformed into a holy restlessness with a clear orientation to God's new creation, with a steadiness of purpose to overcome resistance and frustration. In the words of Rolando Pérez, a sociologist at the Pontifical University in Lima, Peru, "In Latin America, we are still a society that strongly resists looking at those whom we consider to be the *other*. . . . We are profoundly disconnected from our memory, and it is impossible to talk about reconciliation without being connected to our collective memory."[34] A new *we* is not possible without reckoning with the histories of exclusion and violence in which the American Global South was conceived. The groans for a new *we* are the clamor for the recovery of these suppressed memories.

Second, the new *we* being dreamed is a gift before it is a task. It is easy to impose our own vision of beloved community. There is a risk that building for a new *we* creates new exclusions of people or groups who seem problematic in that construction and who should thus be discarded. The attempts to build national unity in Latin America by centering the experience of the mestizo led to the marginalization of peoples of African and Indigenous descent, whose very existence was seen as a throwback to a previous, undesirable era. Therefore, even if the vision of new creation orients the longing for reconciliation, this vision must always be interrogated by the questions of *history*.[35] What is going on? How did we get here?

---

[33] Visit Iniciativa de las Américas at iaptr.com for more information about this initiative.

[34] From *A Vision Towards Peace, Justice, and Reconciliation in the Americas: A Collection of Readings and Discussion Guides from the First Americas Institute for Transformation and Reconciliation (2020–2021)*, ed. Vilma "Nina" Balmaceda (produced by the Center for Reconciliation at Duke Divinity School and the Americas Initiative for Transformation and Reconciliation, 2021), 4. Henceforth *AVTP*.

[35] See also Jennings, "Race and the Educated Imagination," 63.

The gift of the vision of new creation and the gift of the tears of lament must be received together.

Not everyone appreciates this combination of gifts. César Lopes, a Brazilian educator and dean of CETI Continental, has heard colleagues point out how "it is common to discredit the need of grieving as part of the search for justice and the practice of ethics in social relations. This attitude not only cloaks pain and loss, it also eliminates possibilities of reconciliation with life. It is rarely common to be astonished by violence."[36] The language of lament is richly present in Scripture and Christian liturgy, but it has been lost to many in the church. Lopes observes that "the tendency that we see today is that these texts of lament from the Old Testament are simply ignored. In my community and in many other faith communities, we go through a deep denial of suffering. We have removed lament from Christian life."[37] Without lament, the new *we* lacks historical roots.

Third, the new *we* being dreamed is centered in Christ's journey with the peoples of Indigenous and African descent. Jocabed Solano, director of Memoria Indígena and a member of the Guna Dule people of Panama and Colombia, asked the following question to us from her people: "What about us, as part of the body of Christ?"[38] Historically, the voices of the Indigenous have not been heard. Their gifts have not been appreciated in part because of lack of interest in listening to their witness in their own native tongues. Solano explains that "the concept of reconciliation does not exist in the languages of many indigenous peoples. Therefore, how can you talk about an issue that is not even part of the language?"[39]

Solano offered us two gifts from her Guna Dule community to the work of reconciliation. First, she offered the gift of prioritizing the concept of *dules*, which can be translated as *peoples* but also includes the trees and the rivers. She notes how "the Spanish language speaks of us as *nosotros* (*us* and *others*), but the indigenous language speaks of the living being that lives in a common space where we live to commune together." Second,

---

[36] *AVTP*, 26.
[37] *AVTP*, 27.
[38] *AVTP*, 11.
[39] *AVTP*, 6.

Solano offered the gift of a new metaphor for reconciliation: the balanced house. "If we touch a part of something, we touch the whole . . . Or in the simpler words of my Guna Dule grandfather, which are no less profound, we understand that we are living life in harmony when 'our house is in balance.'"[40]

Fourth, the new *we* being dreamed is fragile. We struggle to maintain our vision of the end when bombarded by the polarizing ideologies of the present. It is difficult to heed both the call to unity in Christ and the cry of the poor Christ.[41] The Jesus/Justice divide present in many churches in the United States is also present in the American Global South and indeed around the world. One example stands out in my mind. While teaching a seminar on the theology of reconciliation in the Amazon, I met pastors who were active in community organizations working for land reform. When I asked them how often they had ever preached on this topic from the pulpit, they said, "Never." The connection between the Sunday gospel and the daily advocacy was not obvious. We must learn, practice, and sustain a more holistic vision in the face of polarizing forces.

Fifth, the new *we* dreamed by the Global South first blooms in the peripheries, among the vulnerable and wounded. Drew Jennings-Grisham, one of the co-founders of Memoria Indígena, says it well. "When we consider the Indigenous or Native peoples of our continent, the first sign of hope I see is simply that they are still here. Indigenous resistance in the face of so many centuries of colonization and of attempts to dominate, eliminate, or control their lives and bodies, their knowledge and beliefs, is in itself a sign of hope and liberation."[42] The margins offer rich, fertile ground for hope and liberation, which also means that the new *we* is always endangered. However, the witness of her Indigenous ancestors' persistence encourages Aymara evangelicals such as Juana Luisa Condori Quispe to find hope. "As wounded as

---

[40]*AVTP*, 6-7. Meriting further exploration, this resonates with the language of the earth as our common home found in Pope Francis's encyclical *Laudato si'* (May 24, 2015), available at www.vatican.va/content/francesco/en/encyclicals/documents/papa-francesco_20150524_enciclica-laudato-si.html.

[41]See also Rubén Rosario Rodríguez, "Political Theology as Liberative Theology," *Political Theology* 19, no. 8 (December 2018): 675-80, at 676.

[42]*AVTP*, 39.

the land may be by centuries of oppression, consolation and wise counsel always spring from their wisdom, in a way that is congruent with the written word. That despite how dry and arid the Bolivian *altiplano* (highlands) may feel or look, nourishment and life always spring from it. Certainly, the Spirit blows where He wills."[43]

Despite everything that has happened and is happening, this Aymara evangelical still dreams of finding her identity in the Christ who pitched his tent and dwelt among the Aymara people. The Spirit still blows in the Andean *altiplano*, the Amazonian jungle, the Brazilian *favela*, and the New York barrio. These are dreams from the American Global South, longing for reconciliation and a new, more just *we*.

A PENTECOST JOURNEY

What do these dreams from the American Global South have to do with mentoring Millennial scholars for the North American academy? In a word, *everything*, because Christian education happens after Pentecost in a world where God continues to pour God's Spirit on all flesh, and people of all generations still dream dreams. The dreams from the American Global South are the dreams of many in the North: dreams of better roads connecting the theological academy to the church and the world, dreams of less culturally taxing commutes for underrepresented minorities, dreams of a new, theological *we*.

One of the most important ecclesial signs from the American Global South is the sign of a new Pentecost. A new Pentecost was a reality among mainline Protestant congregations such as the Methodists of Chile, who experienced charismatic renewal in the 1940s, leading to the explosive growth of their membership and witness. The Roman Catholic Church spoke of a new Pentecost as early as the landmark gathering of Catholic bishops in Medellín in 1968 and as recently as the first Catholic ecclesial assembly of Latin America and the Caribbean in 2021.[44]

---

[43]*AVTP*, 45.

[44]See *Documento para el Discernimiento: Todos somos misioneros en salida* (Ciudad de México: Consejo Episcopal Latinoamericano), 2021.

The renewal of the theological enterprise, Amos Yong explains, calls for reclaiming its Pentecost context.[45] Since the church is on a Pentecost journey, the academy must follow along the same path if it is to resource the mission. Traversing this path does not mean schools should teach more courses on missions (though that would be a good start). What is more important is adopting a missiological approach for education as a whole that interprets research, teaching, and service priorities in the light of a Spirit-empowered reading of the gospel and the signs of the times. After Pentecost, mentoring for the academy requires cultivating a new *sentir con la iglesia* (sensing with the church) in the academy, a *sentir* that suffers with those who suffer and dreams with those who dream.

On this Pentecost journey, mentoring for mission entails learning the discourses and accents from a range of academic disciplines, which the Holy Spirit also uses to illuminate truths about God's world, without losing one's own theological accent. The renewal of the theological village happens through a *mestizaje* of peoples and disciplines, including non-theological disciplines. At the same, we must take care along this path. The interdisciplinary approach of the secular academy is guided by a commitment to the pursuit of truth measured by Enlightenment criteria, whereas the Christian academy should be led by the Spirit of truth "to comprehend the truthful interconnected nature of all things in Christ."[46]

Mentoring pilgrims for the Pentecost journey from the theological academy attends to the continuous re-centering of the scholar's vocation. The new *we* is ecclesial; it is constituted through participation in Christ's mission by the power of the Spirit. In other words, the Christian scholar's

---

[45]Amos Yong, *Renewing the Church by the Spirit: Theological Education After Pentecost* (Grand Rapids, MI: Eerdmans, 2020).

[46]Yong, *Renewing the Church*, 103. Yong sees analogues of the experience of xenolalia and interdisciplinarity. He affirms that "the outpouring of the Spirit also involves the empowering of many disciplines, each understood as a set of discursive practices developed and refined over time that enables a dynamic community of inquiry in their inhabitation and exploration of the world" (101). Yong frames his approach in contradistinction to that of Lamin Sanneh. Yong regards Sanneh's translation paradigm as potentially complicit with colonial expansion. For this reason, Yong advocates for theological education after Pentecost to move from translation to interdisciplinary and multidiscursive paradigms. Leaving aside the fairness of Yong's critique of Sanneh, the possibility of Spirit-empowered, Christ-formed multidisciplinary discourse merits serious engagement.

vocation should not be self-referential but apostolic; its intellectual horizon is not the academy but the world, especially its social and existential peripheries. After Pentecost, mentoring involves the formation of habits and postures of dialogue that encounter people in their daily realities with confidence and courage—or what Paul calls *parrhesia*.[47] This confidence comes from listening and discerning the Spirit and the signs of the times *en conjunto* with those who historically have been marginalized from the academy. In this sense, the new *we* is catholic and intentionally inclusive of the voices (and dreams) of mothers and fathers from the early church and of sisters and brothers from the global church. Mentoring for this apostolic and catholic *we* can happen in the North American academy in two complementary ways.

On the one hand, mentoring can happen at "home" by forming people with an eye for opportunities to increase the accessibility of the *we* that constitutes the theological academy. No cultural group has the complete view of God. Only by expanding the theological *we* and entering into dialogue with other cultures as equals can anyone attain a fuller understanding of God.[48] The ease of flow of European ideas in comparison to Latin American ideas is not because there are better ideas in the North than in the South, but because years of faculty and student exchanges have built better roads for them. Including the American Global South in the imagination of our community does not mean bypassing the local. The diaspora communities from the American Global South are our neighbors.

On the other hand, mentoring can happen on the road by, for example, literally riding on buses with people from the American Global South. The dislocations of travel afford the opportunity to consider home with fresh eyes. Journeying together can be transformative. The conversations, the

---

[47] As in 2 Corinthians 3:12; 7:4.

[48] Pope Francis strikes a similar note in *Querida Amazonia*: "Identity and dialogue are not enemies. Our own cultural identity is strengthened and enriched as a result of dialogue with those unlike ourselves. Nor is our authentic identity preserved by an impoverished isolation. Far be it from me to propose a completely enclosed, a-historic, static 'indigenism' that would reject any kind of blending (*mestizaje*)." Pope Francis, *Querida Amazonia*, post-synodal apostolic exhortation (February 2, 2020), sec. 37, see the Vatican website at www.vatican.va/content/francesco/en/apost_exhortations/documents/papa-francesco_esortazione-ap_20200202_querida-amazonia.html.

shared meals, the bumps on the road, the unplanned stops, and the common destination can change the relationship of hosts and guests, students and faculty, into that of fellow pilgrims. The new *we* formed on the road can outlast the common journey on the bus. Sisters and brothers in Christ in Central America now have names and stories. The provinciality of one's own theological village and the challenges of accessibility can be seen more clearly with the benefit of social distance and the development of a spirituality of the way, a bus mystagogy.

I conclude by returning to the bus with which I began. In on our journeys in theological education in Central America, border crossings are an integral part of the journey. The border crossing at Las Chinamas is one that our Guatemalan students have at times found difficult to cross. At Las Chinamas, a bridge crosses over the Paz River, which winds its way between Guatemala and El Salvador. The roads on the Guatemalan side of the border are lonely, and vehicles are notoriously at risk of highway robbers. Sometimes our students have forgotten to bring their migratory documentation, causing delays and headaches in transit. For some of our students, crossing the bridge from Guatemala to El Salvador means crossing significant language and cultural divides from the Indigenous communities where they live to the mestizo communities where they study.

Borders are places of encounter and alienation. For these reasons, our bus school regularly makes a stop at the border, where we gather for worship and renew our baptism at the Paz River. The baptismal *we* is the source of our new *we* and the beginning of our Pentecost journey in a fractured world. At the end of the day, mentoring Millennials (or anyone else) for a diverse academy is simply a baptismal mystagogy that renews dreams of a more just, more inclusive, more Christ-centered *we*.

5

BOOMERS TO ZOOMERS

Mentoring Toward Human Centeredness in Our Work

REBECCA C. HONG

If you've attended a leadership conference or a panel session of organizational leaders, you've likely heard someone ask the question, "What do you do to maintain work-life balance?" Leadership journals and articles have regularly addressed this perennial topic of maintaining a healthy work-life balance, but few have managed to come to an agreed-upon definition of what it means or how to achieve it. Some have claimed that the secret to work-life balance is to regularly take vacations and avoid checking email in the evenings. Others have asserted that if you love what you do, it no longer feels like work; therefore, finding balance is no longer an issue.

Throughout history, laws were established to limit the amount of time people were at work. In the late 1800s, manufacturing laws were established to limit and protect the amount of time women and children worked. By 1938, the Fair Labor Standards Act established a forty-four-hour work week, though medical professionals and doctors exceeded that threshold when "on call."[1] In the 1980s, the women's liberation movement supported women in the workforce, flexible working schedules, and maternity leave to ensure women could both have a career outside the home and continue caring for their families. To date, work-life balance has been the topic of

---

[1]Siva Raja and Sharon L. Stein, "Work-Life Balance: History, Costs, and Budgeting for Balance," *Clinics in Colon and Rectal Surgery* 27, no. 2 (2014): 71-74, www.ncbi.nlm.nih.gov/pmc/articles /PMC4079063/.

hundreds of books, conference sessions, and requests for career and life coaches. Yet an agreed-on definition for the term remains elusive.

The term *work-life balance* assumes there's a magic formula, a perfect ratio that every person can achieve to attain some level of satisfaction in their personal and professional life. In actuality, the amount of energy and engagement, rather than time, varies from person to person. Less variable is what happens when people experience a sense of imbalance between their work and personal lives. Researchers have found that work-life imbalance leads to emotional or physical exhaustion, disconnection, or ineffectiveness.

The blurring of boundaries between work and personal home life became a collective experiment for many people as a result of the coronavirus pandemic and the emergency shift to remote work across many industries. Mentoring practices, and especially mentoring practices designed to serve younger colleagues in higher education, need to consider that the result of this shared experiment has surfaced new and reinvigorated conversations around where, when, and how we work, pushing past the paradox of work-life balance and toward work-life integration that is human centered through leveraging technology.

REMOTE AND FLEXIBLE WORK

Technological advances that opened the door for remote and flexible work environments that are human centered, empowering people to work wherever and whenever, existed prior to the pandemic. Software companies have led the way, leaning in to this work culture, alongside a handful of colleges with large portfolios of online programs even before the pandemic.

Studies conducted prior to the pandemic signaled a growing desire among workers for remote and flexible options. In a 2019 study of eleven thousand workers and sixty-five hundred business leaders, researchers found that remote and flexible work was increasing in popularity among workers desiring better work-life balance, a force for business leaders to address in preparing for the future of work.[2]

---

[2]J. Fuller et al., "Future Positive: How Companies Can Tap into Employee Optimism to Navigate Tomorrow's Workplace," BCG Henderson Institute, Harvard Business School, www.hbs.edu/managing-the-future-of-work/Documents/research/Future%20Positive%20Report.pdf.

The oldest Millennials have grown up immersed in technology, having wireless internet access and immediate communication sources at their fingertips. Younger Millennials cannot recall a time when someone was unreachable by text or instant messaging. Why then does one need to come sit in an office to work? Millennials that entered academia over the past decade as faculty and staff may have encountered this dissonance as the majority of college campuses have not evolved their workplace practices to maximize technological advances.

For example, when a faculty member signs a contract, gets a new ID card, and is issued a university-issued computer, IT departments typically ask for computer preferences: PC or Mac and desktop or laptop? Nearly every faculty member I knew requested a laptop. The mere option of a laptop signals that work can be done anywhere outside an office, whether from home, a local coffee shop, or while traveling. Work happens everywhere and anywhere one determines is suitable to power up the laptop and log in to work.

Specifically in academia, the boundaries between work and home are increasingly porous. It's not uncommon for faculty to be scheduled to teach courses starting at 7:30 a.m. or 7 p.m. on weekdays, Saturdays, never on Fridays, or entirely online. The academic environment has grown increasingly less prescriptive in defining work hours, causing academics to define for themselves the balance between work and personal life. For nonfaculty, the pandemic has shown that many positions have the potential to become remote and flexible; whether they will become so hinges on how organizations embody and view the role of technology to create the future of work. To understand the difference between workplaces that layer technology onto work and workplaces that integrate technology to create a culture that allows people and organizations to find new approaches to how, when, and where work is done, it is critical to first frame the relationship between Millennials and technology.

DIGITAL NATIVES OR JUST TECH SAVVY?

Millennials have often been referred to as "digital natives," having been born between 1981 and 1996, as rapid advancements in technology shaped their daily lives. In 1981, the IBM Personal Computer (PC) was released, demarcating this new generation. In 1987 when the first Millennials were six years old, PowerPoint, a novel presentation software, burst onto the scene, influencing the future of many class presentations to come. By 1993, email entered our public lexicon, replacing the term *electronic mail*, and rapid adoption and use of this new form of communication became the norm.

The first Millennials navigated their high school and college years with a Google search engine, Wi-Fi, disruption of the music industry with Napster and Apple's iPod, and the beginning of social media platforms such as Friendster and later MySpace. As emerging postcollege working professionals, older Millennials entered the workforce and were natural early adopters of first-generation iPhones, cloud-based collaboration tools, and social media platforms such as Twitter and Instagram to create content, find connections, and source information. By 2013, 50 percent of adults in the United States who banked online were Millennials who never had to step foot in a bank to deposit a paycheck.

According to the 2019 Pew Research on generational technology usage, Millennials have consistently been heavier tech adopters and users compared to previous generations.[3] Ninety-three percent of Millennials own smartphones, and 85 percent use social media. Although Millennial use of social media has not significantly changed since 2012, older generations have all increased their use by at least 10 percent during this period of time. As older Americans gradually catch up with technology adoptions and usage, advanced by the pandemic, Millennials may no longer be known for using technology more, but rather differently.

HOW WE WORK

In 2012, Google Docs launched and was quickly popularized for its real-time collaborative functions. No longer did you need to open a Word document, turn on track changes to edit, save the document, and email the attachment back to your teammates. The simultaneous editing function allowed collaborators to seamlessly work together in the cloud as

---

[3]Emily A. Vogels, "Millennials Stand Out for Their Technology Use, but Older Generations Also Embrace Digital Life," Pew Research Center, September 9, 2019, www.pewresearch.org/fact-tank/2019/09/09/us-generations-technology-use/.

anonymous quirky animals without worry of losing the document. In the past ten years, a new generation of collaborative tools (Slack, Microsoft Teams, Asana, GitHub) emerged with expanded features allowing for persistent communication streams, integrated and real-time information sharing, and project management capabilities, all positioned for a new work culture. Although tech companies and startups predominantly staffed by Millennials were the power users of these software tools, the ability to collaborate with coworkers and teammates from anywhere at any time expanded the possibility of a distributed workforce.

Prior to the pandemic, companies such as Dell and SAP offered remote working opportunities and flexible capabilities to employees, positioning themselves to attract the best talent. Companies were positioning themselves for the future of work, one in which work can be done anywhere, anytime. Currently, companies such as WeWork, founded in 2010 with locations both globally and in major cities across the United States, offer office solutions to companies by leveraging their "office" footprint and providing a flexible workplace solution for any employee who works remotely, away from company headquarters. The notions of work being defined as or by a specific location and place are not only disappearing but increasingly less attractive. Yet, according to the 2021 Deloitte Global Millennial and Gen Z Survey, 45 percent of Millennials and Gen Z employees never worked remotely prior to the pandemic.[4]

In a study of Millennials and what they desire out of a workplace, the researcher found that while companies desire employee loyalty, Millennials were significantly more attracted to jobs where there was a high work-life balance.[5] However, employees are growingly skeptical whether their personal definition of work-life balance is possible when expectations of daily commutes to the office are expected and remote and flexible work are not options.

---

[4]"A Call for Accountability and Action: The Deloitte Global 2021 Millennial and GenZ Survey," Deloitte, 2021, www2.deloitte.com/content/dam/Deloitte/global/Documents/2021-deloitte -global-millennial-survey-report.pdf.

[5]John S. Buzza, "Are You Living to Work or Working to Live? What Millennials Want in the Workplace," *Journal of Human Resources Management and Labor Studies* 5, no. 2 (December 2017): 15-20, http://dx.doi.org/10.15640/jhrmls.v5n2a3.

The strictures of being confined to living within a reasonable commute from the office force many to sacrifice personal activities such as time with family and friends, sleep, and exercise. According to the US Census Bureau, the average one-way commute to work increased in 2019 to an all-time high of 27.6 minutes.[6] An average worker is on the road an hour a day, five hours a week, and more than two hundred hours (that's twenty-five eight-hour workdays!) a year. Those who reported their commute of sixty minutes or longer increased from 7.9 percent in 2006 to 9.8 percent in 2019. The benefits of shorter commutes mean more time for rest.

Additionally, according to the US Centers for Disease Control and Prevention (CDC), a third of adults get fewer than seven hours of sleep, the recommended minimum amount each night.[7] Further, research shows that not getting enough sleep is linked to chronic diseases and health risks, depression, motor vehicle crashes, and mistakes at work. Although time spent commuting to work does not directly impact the amount of sleep one might get, the additional time in the day offers people the opportunity to rest, connect, and play.

THE END OF OFFICE LIFE

In 2019, the *New York Times* published an article titled "Young People Are Going to Save Us from Office Life." Millennials and Gen Z have had a front-row seat watching their parents struggle with inflexible workplaces and unstable jobs. Many Millennials witnessed their parents lose jobs, homes, and savings during the Great Recession in 2008, influencing the amount of loyalty they're willing to give their employers.[8] Further, Millennials were also the first generation raised by women who entered the professions in significant numbers.[9] These critical inflection points are key to

[6]"Census Bureau Estimates Show Average One-Way Travel Time to Work Rises to All-Time High," US Census Bureau, March 18, 2021, www.census.gov/newsroom/press-releases/2021/one-way-travel-time-to-work-rises.html.

[7]"Sleep and Sleep Disorders," Centers for Disease Control and Prevention, April 15, 2020, www.cdc.gov/sleep/index.html.

[8]Claire Cain Miller and Sanam Yar, "Young People Are Going to Save Us All from Office Life," *New York Times*, September 20, 2019, www.nytimes.com/2019/09/17/style/generation-z-millennials-work-life-balance.html.

[9]Claire Cain Miller, "More Than Their Mothers: Young Women Plan Career Pauses," *New York Times*, July 22, 2015, www.nytimes.com/2015/07/23/upshot/more-than-their-mothers-young-women-plan-career-pauses.html.

understanding how Millennials may come to form their relationship with work.

Gallup's 2016 study on how Millennials want to work and live found that 55 percent were not engaged at work, as defined by indifference about their job or company.[10] The percentage of Millennials that expressed lower engagement at work was comparatively higher than previous generations. However, the study found that indifference does not equate to entitlement, a ubiquitous description of Millennials. Rather, this study raises the question of whether companies and organizations have reflected on the disconnect between workplace cultures and practices that are fueling disengagement among the biggest generation in the workforce and may lead to burnout, distrust, and resignation.

ERASING THE BOUNDARIES BETWEEN WORK AND HOME: AN UNPLANNED EXPERIMENT

In March 2020 as the novel coronavirus cases escalated across the nation, colleges and universities quickly shifted on-campus courses to remote learning, students moved out of on-campus housing, and faculty and staff frantically packed up their offices and began working off campus. In an instant, kitchen tables were transformed into workspaces, video conferencing headsets, ring lights, and backdrops became work essentials, and work pants became optional! The natural boundaries between work and home and the daily commute to work no longer existed for the majority of workers. The hurried pace of walking across a campus for class, followed by a departmental meeting, stopping to greet a colleague or student, and barely making it in time for a committee meeting vanished. Those routines were replaced by clicking on the Zoom meeting link, seeing familiar faces in boxes on one's computer screen, reminding colleagues that they're on mute, and hitting the leave-meeting button.

Although many campuses adopted learning management systems and video conferencing software prior to the pandemic, the escalating use of these technological tools completely changed how, when, and where we

---

[10]"How Millennials Want to Work and Live," Gallup, Inc., 2016, https://enviableworkplace.com/wp-content/uploads/Gallup-How-Millennials-Want-To-Work.pdf.

worked. Colleges lent employees and students laptops to use, Wi-Fi hotspots for those with slow or no internet at home, and stipends for purchasing any additional equipment to ensure the continuity of work. Despite having the technological capabilities to work away from a physical office, some faced a steep technological learning curve during this time; others found the transition to remote work a potentially exciting experiment. An unplanned effect of this forced remote-work experiment was the burnout that transpires when technology creates flexibility in when and where we work, but organizations fail to change practices around how we work.

BURNOUT

In 2019, the World Health Organization (WHO) updated its handbook of diseases to recognize workplace "burnout" (QD85) as an occupational phenomenon and legitimate medical diagnosis. The WHO describes burnout as "a syndrome conceptualized as resulting from chronic workplace stress that has not been successfully managed. It is characterized by these three dimensions: (1) feelings of energy depletion or exhaustion; (2) increased mental distance from one's job, or feelings of negativism or cynicism related to one's job; and (3) a sense of ineffectiveness and lack of accomplishment."[11]

In October 2020, *The Chronicle of Higher Education* conducted a survey of 1,122 faculty at four-year and two-year institutions on the impact of the coronavirus pandemic on faculty well-being and career plans. Survey findings revealed that since the start of 2020, half of faculty respondents said their enjoyment of teaching had decreased, and more than half felt very stressed compared to the prior year.[12]

The feelings of stress throughout the pandemic have been felt broadly across multiple workforce sectors, and the survey illuminated the impact of this stress and the future of the academic vocation. More than one-third of the faculty surveyed considered changing careers and leaving higher education. Tenured faculty members were the group with the highest

---

[11]"ICD-11 for Mortality and Morbidity Statistics," World Health Organization, May 2021, https://icd.who.int/browse11/l-m/en#/http://id.who.int/icd/entity/129180281.

[12]"On the Verge of Burnout: COVID-19's Impact on Faculty Wellbeing and Career Plans," *Chronicle of Higher Education*, 2020, https://connect.chronicle.com/rs/931-EKA-218/images/Covid%26FacultyCareerPaths_Fidelity_ResearchBrief_v3%20%281%29.pdf.

percentage (43) expressing consideration of leaving the profession. Considering the amount of time and work it requires to become a tenured faculty member, this finding reveals the level of burnout faculty were facing.

For many women, the pandemic also presented compounding new challenges that deteriorated work-life balance at a higher rate than was experienced by men. More female faculty than male faculty noted that an increased workload involving household responsibilities and childcare affected their overall stress level. In a study on the impact of the coronavirus pandemic on the productivity of academics who mother, Kasymova and colleagues denoted the challenges of meeting institutional expectations for research productivity and the challenges of working and teaching online without sufficient institutional support.[13]

In an academic environment where clear delineations of when and where work is completed did not exist prior to the pandemic, compounded with the new levels of exhaustion faculty and staff have faced due to new demands from remote teaching, delays in research, increased demands on time and labor in the home, and emotional tolls from a rolling and seemingly never-ending pandemic, burnout has reached a new level.

But for those who may not be experiencing despondency and a complete depletion of energy, what might signal the potential for burnout? Adam Grant in a *New York Times* piece writes about the feeling between depression and flourishing that was identified by sociologist Corey Keyes. Grant labels this feeling as "languishing" and describes it as "the neglected middle child of mental health." Despite the arrival of vaccines in 2021 that brought new hope, languishing was the dominant emotion of 2021 and then on into 2022 with the emergence of the Omicron variant.[14]

In 2021, many of my fellow academics felt that languishing and burnout impacted their motivation, creativity, inspiration, and hope for their future. Professors, staff, and academic leaders questioned their calling to and the

---

[13]Salima Kasymova et al., "Impacts of the COVID-19 Pandemic on the Productivity of Academics Who Mother," *Gender, Work, and Organization* 28, no. 2 (July 2021): 419-33. Wiley Online Library, https://doi.org/10.1111/gwao.12699.

[14]Adam Grant, "There's a Name for the Blah You're Feeling: It's Called Languishing," *New York Times,* April 19, 2021, www.nytimes.com/2021/04/19/well/mind/covid-mental-health-languishing .html.

future of higher education, and many began exploring careers outside academia. Many women felt attracted to a workplace that featured flexibility and remote work in conjunction with greater support for working parents. Many colleges eagerly messaged their "return to normal" in the fall of 2021, offering limited or even no options for remote flexibility for many employees. This hurried desire to call employees back to work in the office raises several questions: Has there been a missed opportunity to reflect on what was learned about what no longer resonates with a large majority of the workforce? How can the future of work leverage technology while making us more connected as humans? What is at stake if we miss the opportunity to reimagine how, where, and when we work to cultivate a new work culture? What are the ramifications of failing to do so?

THE GREAT RESIGNATION

Anthony Klotz, organizational psychologist and associate professor of management at Texas A&M University, coined the phrase *the Great Resignation* as he examined data on labor turnover as it intersected with the burgeoning of the pandemic.[15] He noticed that the number of people quitting their jobs paused during the early pandemic, signaling a potential bottleneck of employees who wanted to leave their work but were waiting it out. In August 2021, the US Bureau of Labor and Statistics announced that 2.9 percent or 4.3 million Americans quit their jobs, a record-breaking number that has surged past previous months of record numbers.[16]

One common explanation for the current Great Resignation points to the twenty months during the worst of the pandemic when people holed up in their homes and reevaluated what they wanted out of work and life. Workers in America were facing an existential crisis as they faced death and illness around them, many experiencing it close to home. Those moments gave rise

---

[15]Juliana Kaplan, "The Psychologist Who Coined the Phrase 'Great Resignation' Reveals How He Saw It Coming and Where He Sees It Going." *Business Insider*, October 2, 2021, https://www.businessinsider.com/why-everyone-is-quitting-great-resignation-psychologist-pandemic-rethink-life-2021-10.

[16]"Job Openings and Labor Turnover," US Bureau of Labor Statistics, October 12, 2021, www.bls.gov/news.release/archives/jolts_12082021.htm.

to questions around life's purpose, happiness, and reflections that became fuel for life and career pivots. Ulrike Malmendier, UC Berkeley economist, also suggests something existential that the Great Resignation has surfaced: the rise of remote work has changed our view of work.[17]

In higher education, questions concerning whether institutions have employees' interests at heart are accelerating an exodus. Disillusionment with how college leaders handled the pandemic, the racial reckoning across the country, low morale, inadequate compensation, inflexible work practices and a disconnect between personal values and the values espoused by workplaces are also fueling resignations. In a poll conducted by Educause on March 1, 2022, among staff working in higher education, 38 percent of respondents were strongly considering leaving their current institutions for a position elsewhere or had already accepted a position outside their institution. The top two institutional reasons for leaving were poor leadership and lack of resources. Key personal reasons for leaving included desiring more income, better job opportunities, a desire to branch out, wanting improved remote work options, and desiring better work-life policies.[18]

With Millennials comprising a large share of the workforce across academic affairs and student affairs staff, colleges and universities must contend with what this majority of the workforce desires from their work experience. Their expectations are not novel and have been further accelerated by the pandemic. Colleges and organizations are positioned at this time to reexamine institutional policies and practices around when, where, and especially how to engage in work, in order to support, retain, and hire a talented workforce. Institutions cannot afford to underestimate the importance of creating a culture where Millennials can thrive and reinvigorate higher education postpandemic, particularly as the economy faces a surge in worker resignations across nearly all industries.

---

[17]Greg Rosalsky, "Why Are So Many Americans Quitting Their Jobs?" NPR, *Planet Money*, October 19, 2021, www.npr.org/sections/money/2021/10/19/1047032996/why-are-so-many-americans-quitting-their-jobs.

[18]Mark McCormack, "EDUCAUSE Quick Poll Results: The Workforce Shakeup," *Educause Review*, March 4, 2022, https://er.educause.edu/articles/2022/3/educause-quickpoll-results-the-workforce-shakeup.

ENVISIONING THE FUTURE OF WORK:
HUMAN-CENTERED DESIGN

The strain of the pandemic period and the ongoing challenges ahead create conditions for flexibility, creativity, and innovation. As leaders message a "return to work," we must ask what exactly we are returning to, whether workers want to return in person, and what we've learned and reflected on that can shape work in our organizations. We are at an inflection point that requires a deep envisioning of how we work to create future-oriented and people-centered work environments.

If the pandemic has revealed anything, it's that the majority of jobs in the academy can be accomplished from anywhere. As in-person meetings shifted onto Zoom, Slack channels were created, Microsoft Teams was implemented, and in-person courses shifted online, the initial awkwardness quickly subsided as we learned to mute and unmute ourselves, create virtual backgrounds, explore effective online pedagogical strategies, and run remote meetings. The glacial speed by which decisions were historically made in higher education melted as we were forced to quicken our rate of responsiveness in crisis. What we proved to ourselves and the public was that we can indeed be nimble and agile, two words rarely associated with the higher education system prior to the pandemic.

At many institutions the pendulum swung from slow, bureaucratic decision-making cultures to quick, collaborative, and flexible cultures. So how do we now orient our organizations to include what we've learned, how we've been successful, and how people can flourish at work? I posit we consider the possibility of human-centered workplaces.

David Kelley, founder of the global design and innovation company IDEO and Stanford University's Hasso Plattner Institute of Design, also known as the d.school, first popularized the methodology of human-centered design. Human-centered design sits at the intersection of three elements: empathy, creativity, and business needs. In this framework, human-centered designs are fueled by creativity and empathy for people, specifically those who will be using the product. The goal is to find a solution to the problem people are facing by understanding their needs, wants, and desires and, ultimately, to make their lives better.

Leaning into the future of work, considering what we've learned and experienced throughout the pandemic, presents an exciting opportunity for organizations to adopt human-centered approaches to how we design our work environments as we forge through and beyond the pandemic.

Human-centered work: flexibility. How can organizations better understand what work-life balance looks like and, in turn, support this new approach to work? What many organizations have encountered during the pandemic regarding the possibilities of remote work has aligned to what the Deloitte Global Millennial Survey 2020 revealed. Prior to 2020, more than 80 percent of Millennials examined how a particular job would impact their work-life balance, and two-thirds felt remote work provided a better work-life balance. Further, two-thirds of Millennial respondents believed that the option of continuing to work from home after the pandemic would relieve stress in their lives.[19]

Human-centered workplaces design work environments that are attentive and responsive to employees' desires and pain points. For some, the opportunity to work remotely, whether from their homes or from other locations, allowed for opportunities that were never previously possible. Some colleagues noted the opportunity to spend more time with their kids at home and being more present for pivotal moments in their lives. Other colleagues took the opportunity to move to more affordable locations or closer to aging parents or to experience different surroundings. It's critical to note that many Millennials, currently the sandwich generation, are caring for children or aging parents. The phrase *open-faced sandwich generation* can refer to those who care for children or aging parents. This inflection point for the Millennial workforce has escalated the need for employers to be adaptable in terms of the workplace, thus supporting employees' desires and alleviating pain points.

In 2013, a two-year global generational study on Millennial employees of PricewaterhouseCoopers (PwC) highlighted the necessary key changes in the workplace to attract and retain Millennial talent.[20] One key learning

---

[19]"The Deloitte Global Millennial Survey 2020: Resilient Generations Hold the Key to Creating a 'Better Normal,'" Deloitte, 2020, www2.deloitte.com/content/dam/Deloitte/global/Documents /About-Deloitte/deloitte-2020-millennial-survey.pdf.

[20]"PwC's Next Gen: A Global Generational Study," PWC, 2013, www.pwc.com/gx/en/hr-manage ment-services/publications/assets/pwc-nextgen.pdf.

from the study revealed that Millennials viewed work as a thing, some-thing you do, and not a place. You do work, you don't "go" to work; this reflects the expectation of working anywhere and at any time. Further, the study revealed that Millennials believed productivity should be measured by output and outcomes of the work performed, as opposed to the number of hours in the office. When we measure work productivity as hours in the office, it directly contrasts how faculty are reviewed and promoted across ranks. When was the last time faculty were promoted for hours spent on research for a peer-reviewed publication as opposed to the pub-lication of the article itself? Do we evaluate staff for the number of hours they're in the office or for how our students indicate that their needs are being met? The notion that sitting in the office is a better measure of work than output or outcomes of one's work is in direct opposition to what Millennials have expressed.

Assuming work productivity and effectiveness can be achieved only in the office challenges what we've experienced throughout the pandemic. It will be critical for leaders to study and understand what kind of envi-ronment leads to the highest productivity for Millennial faculty and staff, first by asking what workforce outcomes we are hoping to achieve and how best to achieve them. This requires deep trust and understanding of your workforce and an adaptability to diverse approaches to work.

For faculty who have spent eighteen months teaching remotely because of the pandemic, what has been illuminated about effective pedagogical practices? What types of students have thrived in an online environment, and what practices have served them well? What have universities learned about creating equitable learning environments, and how will they con-tinue to adopt these practices for courses continuing online? How can some of these practices be adopted for in-person courses? Answers to these questions require an openness to redesigning work environments and organizational practices.

It's worth scrutinizing what might drive resistance from college leaders to allow remote and flexible work options to continue postpandemic. The reasoning may vary for why colleges have "come-back-to-work policies." Some have pointed to the fear of loss of community and personal connection, only to be replaced by computers and technology. Yet organizational leaders and managers have the opportunity to reimagine how community can be created and the role technology can play to deepen these connections, particularly among generations for which technology and social media are a hallmark imprinted on their daily lives.

Human-centered work: Community and connection. Technology platforms, real-time messaging platforms, video conferencing, and cloud collaboration tools existed prior to the pandemic and allowed us to stay connected in our work throughout the pandemic. These digital tools will continue to expand and be integral to how we work. Investments in technological upgrades during the pandemic have developed infrastructure that will remain with remote and flexible work plans. Traditionally minded academic institutions are shelving available technological infrastructures, seeing them as temporary solutions for emergency remote work during the pandemic; their goal is to bring people back in person to establish community and connection once again.

Thomas Malone, founding director at MIT's Center for Collective Intelligence and author of *Superminds: The Surprising Power of People and Computers Thinking Together*, examines human-digital collaborations. He finds that there isn't a reason to return to a traditional office now that staff know they are able to do their work remotely with the help of computers.[21] Yet the beckoning call back to the office for the purposes of (re)building community and connection has people wondering how sitting masked in a conference room engenders community and connection. Are in-person meetings or unplanned run-ins with colleagues the most effective methods of cultivating community and connection?

What needs to be examined is not a binary argument of whether in-person or remote flexible work fosters greater community and connection. Rather, our desires for community and connection should lead us to address *how* we can intentionally shape and design the purpose and reason for gathering virtually versus gathering in person.

---

[21]Steven Zeitchik, "MIT Expert on Work Says Any Boss Who Thinks Employees Will Return to Office Is Dreaming," *Washington Post*, October 26, 2021, www.washingtonpost.com/technology /2021/10/26/thomas-malone-mit-faq-work/.

Priya Parker, author of *The Art of Gathering: How We Meet and Why It Matters*, notes that there are many good reasons for why we gather, but we often fail to home in on the *why*. Failing to clarify why we are convening people together, undergirded with a clear and communicated purpose, results in gatherings that don't serve us and in deciding not to gather when we ought to.[22] In 2019, Doodle, an online calendaring tool, presented *The State of Meetings Report*, quantifying the cost of pointless meetings. On average, professionals said they spent three hours a week in meetings, two-thirds of those meetings being a waste of time. Pointless meetings cost companies worldwide more than half a trillion dollars per year, with more than a third of professionals viewing pointless meetings as the greatest cost to an organization, not to mention overall employee happiness with work.[23] It's no surprise that numerous social media memes and merchandise post the saying, "This meeting should have been an email."

We are at a critical junction where the opportunity to design a remote and hybrid workforce with purposeful connection and intentional community building can be achieved. An increasing number of organizations with hybrid and remote-first teams are creating community through new approaches. Remote companies have designed annual off-site gatherings or retreats that bring people together for a few days of team building and downtime. Companies such as Zapier, based in California with 350 employees located across the United States and in twenty-three other countries, hold employee annual retreats that last between one day to a full work week, filled with work meetings and fun activities, all with the goal of getting to know one another. Buffer, a software company, went remote in 2015, prior to the pandemic. The company holds annual company retreats lasting about nine days—five days to work, two days prior to arrive and get settled, and the weekend afterward to relax and rest. These two examples of how remote companies are fostering community provide a glimpse of

[22]Priya Parker, *The Art of Gathering: How We Meet and Why It Matters* (New York: Riverhead, 2018), 11.
[23]"The State of Meetings 2019," Doodle, January 10, 2019, https://en.blog.doodle.com/2019/01/10/pointless-meetings-will-cost-companies-530bn-in-2019/.

how organizations can rethink how collective time can be purposefully structured to achieve the goals of community and connection.

If heading toward a remote-first organization is not feasible at this time, organizations can thoughtfully examine how frequently they require in-person meetings and ask if and when meeting online or by hybrid means can achieve the same goals. The *Harvard Business Review* offered this chart (see fig. 5.1) as a starting point when pondering whether to meet in person based on the goals of the meeting.[24]

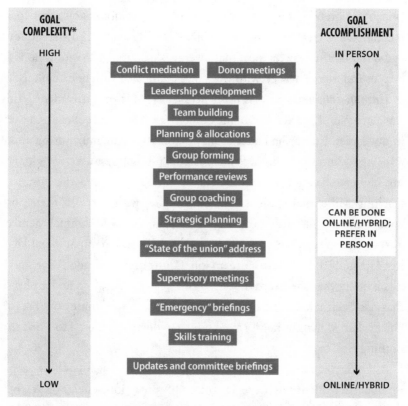

*In this context, "complexity" includes emotional complexity, the range of interdependence, or the need for intervention.

Figure 5.1. Determining whether you need to meet in person

Source: Adapted from Rae Ringel, "When Do We Actually Need to Meet in Person?," *Harvard Business Review*, July 26, 2021. Used by permission.

---

[24]Rae Ringel, "When Do We Actually Need to Meet in Person?," *Harvard Business Review*, July 26, 2021, https://hbr.org/2021/07/when-do-we-actually-need-to-meet-in-person.

The experiment of remote work for traditional companies throughout the pandemic has opened vistas, showing what can be done better in a virtual format. It is incumbent upon organizational leaders and influencers to listen to the experiences of those who have thrived in a remote work format and those who have desired something from work that was not available during the pandemic. There is valuable data across our organizations that point to possibilities of creating new ways of working that reject binary notions of how and when we work. For starters, we can begin by listening and empathizing with what people need from their workplaces. This inflection point for many colleges and organizations allows for experimentation and creativity, excavation of historically unchecked assumptions, and a thoughtful way forward that leverages technological innovations to help us feel more engaged with work and connected with one another.

Human-centered work: Valuing people. What is your dream job? This was a question I heard asked of me quite a bit throughout college and early in my career. I never had a clear answer, only a vague murmuring about wanting to find work that was purposeful and that best used my gifts. In my higher education career as a faculty member, I had the honor of teaching Millennial students and journeying with them in their post-college careers. Recently I connected with one of my Millennial mentees as she was job searching. I asked her what a dream job might look like to her. She said, "I don't have a dream job. I don't dream of labor." She said it was a quote that she heard among those in her generation and a phrase that has been circulating among anticapitalist communities on TikTok. She explained that for her it's a resistance to devoting oneself to work and nothing else.

As I reflected on our conversation, I was reminded again of how deeply influenced Millennials were by the 2008 recession, effects now compounded by the pandemic. They have already witnessed parents lose their jobs and homes after giving so much of themselves to their careers. As they live through a pandemic where some got laid off or have had no option to continue flexible and remote work options despite doing so successfully for more than a year, their skepticism has been reinforced about corporate life. Experiencing inflexible workplaces that put profit over people continues to breed skepticism among the workforce and reinforces distrust in organizations. Inflexible work environments further exacerbated by worker burnout and feelings of being undervalued fuel reasons for resignation.

As indicated in the 2016 Gallup survey "How Millennials Want to Work and Live," one of the top five things Millennials looked for when applying for jobs was the opportunity to learn and grow.[25] Opportunity to grow was also one of the top four things on which Millennials wanted their managers to focus. However, learner was in the top five strengths of all four generations surveyed by Gallup. People are inherently curious and desire to learn.

Human-centered organizations know people are their greatest asset and most critical investment. Developing their own employees, valuing and appreciating the workforce, and providing career pathways for growth help sustain and scale organizations to push past a zero-sum game mentality. Human-centered organizations empower people to flourish through opportunities to learn and grow—from health and wellness to professional skills and career competencies or through formal and informal mentoring opportunities. Valuing people is another human-centered approach to work that provides an opportunity to disrupt ubiquitous perceptions that people are cogs in a wheel and replaceable. It humanizes each person and sees individuals as unique and valuable contributors to an organization.

CONCLUSION

When I was initially asked to write this chapter more than two years ago, I had been following companies that had transitioned to remote teams or started as remote companies. I regularly wondered how higher education could effectively integrate technology to advance our work. At the time, I was commuting at least two hours a day, driving more than fifty miles round trip, to work on campus. I did that for more than eight years before moving to my current institution, where I drive half the distance but nearly the same amount of time on the road.

---

[25]"How Millennials Want to Work and Live."

Prior to moving into administration, I started as a tenure-track faculty member eleven years ago, teaching courses online in our master's programs while advising students virtually. While hardly anything required of faculty teaching online warranted us to step foot on campus, we were required by the department chair to sit in our offices during office hours. Further, our online students rarely stepped foot on campus until graduation day. My department chair would come by regularly and ensure that we were in our offices. I once witnessed my colleague being reprimanded for not being in his office, though he was also teaching only online and held virtual office hours. It never made sense as to why I needed to drive two hours a day to sit in my office, open up my laptop, and meet virtually with my students.

As my role transitioned from faculty to administrator, my days frequently filled with back-to-back meetings. Although the university had adopted WebEx for their video conferencing platform, we never used it for meetings. In fact, we rarely used it except when conducting the initial round of interviews for searches. I often wondered what was preventing us from leveraging the full capacity that technology offered. As many of my colleagues commuted for hours, some by train and then bus, arrived on campus for an 8:30 a.m. meeting, and stayed on campus to teach late into the evening, I often wondered how we might better foster a community of people more deeply connected with themselves, their families, and their broader communities. Why weren't we leveraging existing technology for our meetings and allowing people to avoid morning rush hour, get more sleep, and feel more connected to themselves and their communities? There was nothing we were doing in person that couldn't be done in a remote fashion. Yet it appeared that we were using technology in an additive versus integrative approach, perhaps in a fear-based way, to ensure humans will never be replaced by machines. But something has never seemed right about that approach.

The research shared and the reflections made in this chapter are intended to create conversations around how we can become *more* human by being more intentional and purposeful when we gather for work, whether in person or online, and how we value and empower one another to be more whole people when we work in remote and flexible ways. These are the benefits of collaborating *with* technology.

The pandemic has accelerated these conversations around the future of work and how to create human-centered organizations that provide flexibility and connection and value their people. Although much of this chapter examined data from Millennials and what they desire out of work, the findings and practices can be applied across generations.

6

INTENTIONAL INFLUENCE

*Relevant Practices and Habits We Must Cultivate
in Today's Emerging Generation*

TIM ELMORE

I chuckled at a one-frame comic that showed a young, longhaired college student, who was sporting a beard, several tattoos, and flip-flops, speaking to his father, seated in an easy chair in the living room. The student explained his lifestyle to his dad, "But, Dad, I gotta be a nonconformist if I'm gonna be like everyone else!"

Such are the sentiments of young adults of each generation over the past sixty years. We all wanted to be different, and we all wanted to fit in. We all felt we were unique, as if we were discovering realities no one had discovered before. In some ways, history does repeat itself. There are certain cycles that appear within culture as each new iteration of humans matures into adulthood. Perhaps Rafiki in *The Lion King* was right when he said there is a "circle of life."

BUT IS THERE REALLY A GENERATION GAP?

People often ask me why I make an issue of the different generations on campus today. Is there really a disparity between them, or are the differences merely about life stages? In short, isn't every generation of teens basically the same but just growing up in different times?

Certainly adolescents and young adults in every generation share similar characteristics—their brains are maturing but not fully developed. Consequently a "gap" has always existed between the old and the young.

And the elders usually complain about the immaturity of the kids. More than twenty-four hundred years ago, Socrates mourned the state of youth in his day:

> Children now love luxury; they have bad manners, contempt for authority; they show disrespect for elders and love chatter in place of exercise. Children are now tyrants, not the servants of their households. They no longer rise when elders enter the room. They contradict their parents, chatter before company, gobble up dainties at the table, cross their legs and tyrannize their teachers.[1]

The Roman playwright Plautus reportedly quipped, "Manners are always declining." More recently, poet and playwright T. S. Eliot noted, "We can assert with some confidence that our own period is one of decline; that the standards of culture are lower than they were fifty years ago; and that the evidences of this decline are visible in every department of human activity."[2]

The gap today, however, is wider and expanding more rapidly than ever.

The greatest difference between populations of youth has to do with the way technology has evolved over the past sixty years. The term *generation gap* was coined in the 1960s by *Look* magazine editor John Poppy. He noticed that regarding politics, tastes, morals, and virtually everything else, there was a substantial divide between the young and the old—with the "old" including everyone over thirty. Does this sound strangely familiar? The truth is that "generation gaps are hardly a novelty"; indeed, as Pew Research Center author Paul Taylor points out: "Nearly two centuries ago Alexis de Tocqueville marveled that in America 'each generation is a new people.'"[3]

In 2018, the *Global Demographic Report 2018* was prepared by the Insights Research Team. It was a mammoth study involving people from four generations (Gen Z, Millennials, Gen X, and Baby Boomers). The research included more than half a million individuals (561,507 to be

---

[1] Quoted in William L. Patty and Louise S. Johnson, *Personality and Adjustment* (New York: McGraw-Hill, 1953), 277.

[2] T. S. Eliot, *Notes Towards the Definition of Culture* (London: Faber & Faber, 1948).

[3] Paul Taylor, *The Next America: Boomers, Millennials, and the Looming Generational Showdown* (New York: PublicAffairs, 2015), 30.

exact) from more than sixty counties and regions around the world. The conclusion? Generations do, indeed, possess personalities. For example, the two younger generations (Millennials and Gen Z) are significantly more social than Baby Boomers. The study used the color schema developed from psychologist Carl Jung and ancient Greek physician Hippocrates, which is built around the four fundamental personality types:

- Fiery Red (choleric)
- Sunshine Yellow (sanguine)
- Cool Blue (melancholy)
- Earth Green (phlegmatic)

One might assume that globally there would be an even distribution of different personalities among each generation. This isn't the case, however, according to the data. Whether due to nature or nurture (or both), personality types vary depending on which generation someone comes from. People younger than twenty-five are almost twice as likely to be Sunshine Yellow (sanguine) than those who are older than sixty, according to the study. Those under twenty-five are social creatures. Although we could argue that this is almost always the case, as young people from every generation tend to lead through social relationships more than older people, it doesn't matter. The fact remains that it is clearly pronounced today. The study revealed a tendency toward extraversion in young adults. Twenty-somethings—thanks to their smartphones—are prone to be connected to others far more often than Gen Xers or Boomers. This may explain why I consistently hear remarks from senior managers that their young team members can't seem to stop talking and start working on the task in front of them. Another finding from the study: those who are older than forty-five are more likely to be Fiery Red (choleric: directive and task oriented) than those who are under forty-five. In fact, that number tends to climb with age—up until senior citizens older than sixty. Although there are clearly different personalities in each generation, younger adults tend to favor social relationships, and older adults tend to favor task orientation.[4]

---

[4]Insights Research Team, *Global Demographic Report 2018*, 9-10, www.insights.com/media/2205/insights-discovery-global-demographic-report.pdf.

In other words, although younger team members tend to lean toward extroversion, introversion is more prominent in older age groups.

This gap may explain what's happening on university campuses and in workplaces today.

WHY IS THE GAP WIDENING?

The goal for this chapter is to define the practices and habits of today's emerging generation of students and then to define what practices and habits they will need to thrive as they enter their careers. To do this, we will benefit from understanding what's causing the changes to their current lifestyles and how to connect with them as mentors, instructors, parents, or coaches. There are actually six different generations living today. From my perspective, generation gaps between them are caused by at least five factors:

- rapid changes in culture
- increased life expectancy
- the mobility of society
- shifting economies
- new technologies and media

One huge factor that has influenced generation gaps is the accelerating rate of change in society. Two hundred years ago, cultural developments were slower. As a result, two or three generations lived lifestyles that were relatively similar to each other. But because of the technological and social advances in the twentieth and twenty-first centuries, the lifestyles of people even one generation apart are measurably different from one another.

Additionally, life spans have increased over the centuries. As people live longer and babies continue to be born, we now have more generations alive at one time than at any other time in modern history. Different paradigms emerge as our minds are exposed to different realities at younger ages. Furthermore, because an older generation's neural pathways were set in a different time period than those of a younger generation, they tend to have different perspectives. Increasing life spans can create more gaps in any population.

Another factor that has influenced the generation gap is our increased mobility. In earlier time periods, society was not nearly as mobile. Most people stayed in the same area or country. There was little contact with people outside of one's general area. Access to information from other cultures was limited. Today most of us have either traveled to or watched a film about different cultures and nations.

Another factor in the narrative of a generation is the shifting economy while they're growing up and preparing for adulthood. Even though young and only indirectly influenced, they watched adults react to the marketplace with caution or confidence in their spending and investments. Notice how the economy correlates with the size and spirit (tone) of each generation. Consider the narrative of the most recent five, shown in table 6.1.

Table 6.1. Economy correlates of the past five generations

The Generation	The Tone	The Economy	The Population
The builders	Caution	Mostly bear market	Smaller
The boomers	Confidence	Mostly bull market	Larger
The busters (Xers)	Caution	Mostly bear market	Smaller
The millennials	Confidence	Mostly bull market	Larger
Gen Z	Caution	Mostly bear market	Smaller

Further, advances of technology have introduced new information and images. Consider the changes in technology that have occurred in the past twenty years. Today children may explain to adults how to use portable devices. They may use different apps on their smartphones to connect with peers, giving them a totally different life experience than an older generation. A young man will choose to spend his time on public transportation texting a friend, while an older man passes the time reading a physical book. It's a picture of the times in which we live.

As I ponder today's widening generation gap, the chief cause appears to be reduced to a single word: *exposure.* Life expectancy, travel, media, and technology all increased exposure to new information and experiences, and this allows for different perspectives. For most of the causes of a generation gap, we can't do much about them—and we don't want to. There is one cause, however, that we *can* influence, and I'd like to reflect on it now.

OUR SCREENS WENT FROM PUBLIC TO PRIVATE

Eighty years ago, there were no screens in the average American home. Families enjoyed radio programs and often listened to broadcasts together. In the 1950s, televisions entered the scene. By 1960, we reached a tipping point. According to the *World Book Encyclopedia*, "By 1960, there were 52 million sets in American homes, which meant a TV in almost nine out of ten households."[5]

Originally, however, television programs were designed like radios, where the entire family would gather in front of the television set to watch shows such as *I Love Lucy* or *The Andy Griffith Show*. By the late 1960s, however, we saw niche marketing, as shows targeted specific audiences. *Sesame Stree*t was a show for preschool children. *Laugh-In* was a prime-time show designed for adults who enjoyed satire. Airing in 1965, *Never Too Young* was the first soap opera geared toward a teen audience. Niche programming further divided adults from kids. In time, media messaging informed each demographic differently. Although there may have been just one television in the home and everyone knew what each person was watching, the information was segmented. Eventually there were multiple television sets in a home, allowing for further segmenting in a family.

Later, when the personal computer was introduced in the 1990s, families became even more segmented. It acted like the television in that there was usually one desktop machine, often in the kitchen, so everyone knew what the others were viewing. This time, however, users could search for content based on their interests. Life became more niche based for each generation. Consumption became both targeted and "on demand."

As the twenty-first century dawned, life changed even more. Our screens moved from public to private. Instead of one screen shared by everyone, it became the norm for each person to have his or her own screen—a smartphone, a tablet, or a laptop. Today, parents may not even know what their teens are consuming. The platforms are in our individual hands, and content is targeted toward different audiences. Everything is niche.

---

[5] *The World Book Encyclopedia*, s.v. "television" (Chicago: World Book, 2003), 119.

Portable devices not only allowed for a more personalized experience, but they also created virtual communities for anyone using them. Social media allows millions of teens, for instance, to create an Instagram account, and perhaps several other Finsta accounts, which allow for fake Instagram personas. Mom and Dad often have no idea they exist.

Author and Emory University professor Mark Bauerlein wrote that teens now network with one another in unique ways wherein they can associate with peers exclusively. They have never lived a life so wholly unto themselves.[6] A hundred years ago, teens might spend as much time with parents, uncles, aunts, and other adults as they did with peers. The gap was smaller as time with multiple generations occurred. Over time, the gap has widened:

- Education migrated from a one-room schoolhouse to graded classrooms where students spend time with only their age demographic, not with multiple age groups.

- Media programming, as I mentioned, has evolved into niche markets, usually based on demographic interests, which foster homogenous communities.

- Faith communities and churches split up attendees into age groups, so families seldom learn or worship together but instead do so in age-targeted audiences.

- Consumers now expect content to be customized for them and don't want to work as hard at translating concepts for application. We've grown socially lazy.

Minimally, this explains why connecting with others is harder work today. We may have little in common with younger people because their personal niche is so different. Connecting with different generations now requires more work to find any overlap or common ground. It may feel like a crosscultural relationship.

---

[6]Mark Bauerlein, *The Dumbest Generation: How the Digital Age Stupefies Young Americans and Jeopardizes Our Future (Or, Don't Trust Anyone Under 30)* (New York: Simon and Schuster, 2009).

THE CURRENT HABITS OF YOUNG ADULTS

Millennials are now in the workforce or have at least graduated from school. Gen Z is the population currently preparing for a career, and members make up the youngest population being studied. The three primary sources of their current habits are

- smart technology—their screens moved from public to private and their lives are niched;

- parents who often risked too little, rescued too quickly, and raved too easily; and

- schools that drifted from the original "career and life-ready" goal to academic scores.

Chap Clark's research at Fuller Seminary reveals that teens have fewer adults in their lives than previous generations. Clark began observing this reality a decade ago in his book *Hurt 2.0*.[7] Consider the impact of his data. If teens or young adults spend less time with adults or have fewer adults making deposits in their minds and hearts, their habits and practices are likely more informed by peers and media. The mentor influencing our son or daughter is less likely to be Socrates or Moses or even Uncle Bob. It's Josh or Emma down the street on Instagram.

Further, I believe this separation informs our opinion of them. Up close, we are more likely to understand them, empathize with them, and know how to lead them. From farther away, our emotions can become negative: suspicion, fear, frustration, or even judgment or prejudice. As research psychologist Brené Brown reminded us, "It is hard to hate people close up."[8]

I had a hunch a few years back about the perspective of adults regarding young people today. I continually saw frustration on the adults' faces and heard impatience in their voices. I witnessed a gap. So our organization, Growing Leaders, partnered with Harris Interactive in 2018 to survey more than two thousand adults from varying backgrounds, ethnicities,

---

[7]Chap Clark, *Hurt 2.0: Inside the World of Today's Teenagers* (Grand Rapids, MI: Baker Academic, 2011).
[8]Brené Brown, *Braving the Wilderness* (New York: Random House, 2019), 63.

ages, genders, and states. We asked them about their view of today's emerging generation. My hypothesis was validated.

Sixty-six percent of American adult respondents admitted a negative rather than a positive emotion when they thought about young people today. Words such as *concern* and *fear* were used more often than *hope* and *excitement*. Similarly, 64 percent of American adults did not believe Gen Z would be ready for adulthood when it is time. Adults assume they'll be unready to assume responsible roles, pay bills, and rise to the challenges of our day. My question is: How must it feel to be parented, taught, coached, and managed by older leaders who experience negative emotions about you and don't believe you'll be ready for the future? Our negative attitude will naturally come out in our verbal, nonverbal, and para-verbal communication. Young adults may soon adopt our narrative—and it becomes a self-fulfilling prophecy. What's more, if young adults are unready to form the right habits and practices, who's to blame? We cannot merely blame our young. They are products of our making. Too often, we have prepared the path for the child instead of the child for the path.

PRACTICES AND HABITS ON THE UNIVERSITY CAMPUS

As Millennials entered college campuses twenty years ago, universities attempted to adjust to these twenty-first-century students. Although scholarship still existed in classrooms, student life was evolving rapidly based on the culture in which those students had grown up. In my observation, the student affairs experience adjusted more rapidly than the academic experience on campus. Below are several practices that the changing students fostered on college campuses.

Attention spans informed the education experience. Attention spans have dropped among adolescents. In the year 2000, teen attention spans were reported to be about twelve seconds long. This did not mean students could not pay attention to something any longer than twelve seconds. After all, these days students often binge-watch a Netflix or Hulu series for hours. It simply meant they paid attention for about twelve seconds before they were distracted or diverted by something more engaging. Today teen attention spans have dropped to eight seconds. In response, professors have attempted to reduce instruction to smaller sections and take breaks for discussion. Student affairs staff will train resident advisers in sound bites, making it very interactive, building from experiential lesson plans. I know some coaches and teachers who take a classroom break for students to get a "social media fix." Right or wrong, student engagement is the first job of the educator. Students get bored quickly.

Social preferences have informed the community experience. Millennials and Gen Zers are connected to peers almost 24/7. Some call them "screenagers," as these young people's daily interactions moved from in-person to a cell phone to a smartphone. Many confess to being addicted to their phones. A Pew Research Center study reported teens are on a screen for almost eight hours a day—the equivalent of a full-time job. It's been said, "When our phones had leashes, we were free. Now our phones are free, and we have leashes." Despite being familiar and comfortable with screens, young adults report preferring face-to-face interactions with teachers, advisers, and employers. This may be due to the long hours spent on Zoom or Google Meet calls during the coronavirus quarantine. This may also be partly because of their desire to be with each other. College campuses have responded by redesigning residence halls to foster community and relationships over isolation.

Mental health issues have informed the counseling and guidance experience. Front and center on the minds of staff and faculty is the poor mental health of university students. First-year students complain of feeling overwhelmed and often find it difficult to function, and suicidal ideation occurs often. In August 2020, the Centers for Disease Control reported that one in four young adults (ages 16-24) contemplated suicide in the previous month. Students are preoccupied with the coronavirus pandemic, protests, panic attacks, pay cuts, polarization, and poor prospects for their future career dreams. Hundreds of campuses report failing to have enough counselors to manage inquiries from their students interested in therapy sessions. More revenue is needed in this field to help students manage their emotions, their priorities, and the onslaught of information coming at them on social media.

Bias toward technology has informed the teaching/learning experience. Students today are digital natives and are at home learning online, surfing the internet, and gaining what they need from YouTube, Wikipedia, and Google searches. In fact, teens are asking Google, Siri, and Alexa questions they used to ask their parents and teachers. Students no longer need us for information. But they do need us for interpretation. We must help them make sense of all they know. They often digest content with no context. They may have viewed several YouTube videos but have only a two-dimensional experience of a topic. They are exposed to information far earlier than they are ready but are exposed to firsthand experiences far later than they are ready. It has often produced what I call *artificial maturity*. An example is a student who knows much about many topics (e.g., math equations, downloading software, fantasy NFL teams) but has little work or life experience, as his or her parents have erred on the side of safety and risk-free activities. Universities have capitalized on students' bias toward screens and now offer a plethora of online learning options.

A consumer mindset has informed the extracurricular experience. University administrators experience a steady flow of parental inquiries, complaints, and suggestions for improving the "customer experience" of their sons and daughters. I recently heard one tenured professor say a student confronted him after receiving a poor grade on a paper. The student argued that his parents had paid full tuition, entitling him to an A. Many families, though certainly not all, view the university experience as a product or service from a vendor. There are many options for their students, so they want the best value possible. Forty years ago, when I attended college, it was the job of the students to learn and to initiate their pursuit of knowledge. Today it is the job of the instructors to ensure students grasp and digest content. Campuses have become more user-friendly and consumer-welcoming in their amenities and food services. *Edutainment* is a term some critics use to describe this new higher education experience. Because of the financial transaction, administrators don't want to lose customers.

Often I hear academicians mourn the lack of discipline in today's youngest generation. These students seem unable to delay gratification and appear to lack ambition and humility. They often don't exhibit critical-thinking skills, and they seem fragile when it comes to receiving hard feedback. Staff and faculty have grieved these realities in the teachers' lounge.

We must remember, however, that students are products of today's culture and the result of our leadership. Our practices must work like a social, emotional, spiritual, and intellectual fitness center. We must ask ourselves: Are the practices and habits that define our campus culture producing career-ready graduates? Do the activities and traditions cultivate adults who are ready for life after graduation? Further, do the practices and habits on campus prepare them for the future in which they will spend the rest of their lives?

TWO META-COMPETENCIES WE MUST CULTIVATE IN STUDENTS

As I gaze across the horizon, I believe there are two meta-competencies that stand above all others. Certainly there are several important skills graduates will need, but two of them seem to be overarching umbrellas, influencing the others when they are present. These meta-competencies are (1) resourcefulness and (2) resiliency.

In 2012, Bradford Smart released his third edition of *Topgrading*. Each edition is full of insights on how to hire, develop, and keep A-players on your team. In the midst of the message, the author suggests that in the world of tomorrow, resourcefulness is king. Let me summarize and explain this message, then apply it to today's students.

Smart writes that resourcefulness is the new meta-competency as employees enter the workforce. Think about it. Because information is ubiquitous, we no longer need people who know a lot. Information is readily available. You can search and find answers to almost any problem if you know where to look. That's why the virtue of resourcefulness is now the most important skill to build and find. Universities must cultivate people who know how to find answers, people who can identify and solve problems because they can find solutions far beyond our current practice. Resourceful people

- can comprehend the key problems that slow down progress,
- practice critical-thinking skills to diagnose and comprehend issues,

- search for and find ideas they can connect to those problems,
- are able to develop a series of solutions to the problems, and
- have the ability to modify and implement the best solutions.[9]

Why do I believe resourcefulness is a meta-competency today? Chiefly because a K-12 student today has a high probability of getting a job after graduation that doesn't even exist today. In fact, it is increasingly probable that they will have not only several jobs but jobs in several industries. Many will claim they'll enjoy several careers, not just one. Each of these will require them to search and find new ways to reinvent themselves.

As teachers facilitate learning for their students, this is a profound truth to recognize. To give students an advantage as they mature into adulthood, we must equip them to be resourceful, to not shrink from digging into issues and drawing conclusions about them, and to know how to search for and find answers for themselves. Certainly, faculty should create classrooms that demand resourcefulness on assignments. I believe student affairs staff must also create labs where students are required to practice resourcefulness to succeed. Our chief hurdle, in my opinion, is this: we take pride in resourcing them so well that they often don't develop any skills in resourcefulness. The most resourceful people are frequently the ones who grew up with fewer resources.

There is one additional valuable competency that we must intentionally build into the lives of students: resilience. Resilience is the ability to bounce back after adversity. The speed and convenience that mark our culture have diminished this virtue. Teachers nationwide report that young people today give up too easily. They don't like problems that take too long or require too much effort to solve. There seems to be an inverse relationship between the following attributes and resources:

- **Options and commitment.** With so many options and opportunities, students sometimes prefer to move on when life gets tough instead of staying committed to their original commitments.

---

[9]Brad Smart, *Topgrading: The Proven Hiring and Promoting Method That Turbocharges Company Performance* (New York: Penguin, 2005).

- **Attention and information**. Herbert Simon said it best: "A wealth of information creates a poverty of attention."[10] If content is ubiquitous, attention spans may be shortened.
- **Speed and longevity.** When results come quickly, patience levels drop. Our on-demand, instant-access culture has created a "microwave" instead of a "slow cooker" expectation.

We surveyed more than eight thousand students in 2016 and discovered resilience is a rare commodity among secondary-school students. Research psychologist Angela Duckworth created a Grit Scale at the University of Pennsylvania that can evaluate as well as compare scores of those who take it.[11] She has shown that today's youth have measurably lower scores than those of older generations. In our surveys, students' top remarks to teachers in K-12 education are:

- "This is too hard."
- "I need help."
- "I can't do this."

Because technology has made life quick and easy, leaders and teachers must find ways to develop resiliency in students. Could it be that current practices and habits failed to prepare them to hunger for what is hard? Does this inform what universities must focus on with students?

THREE MENTORING PRACTICES FOR ADMINISTRATORS

Over the past forty years of my career, I have engaged in mentoring relationships with students and gleaned both what works best and what to avoid. I have also chronicled in my journal "best practices" administrators have implemented to form developmental relationships with their "end users." I offer them here.

---

[10]Herbert Simon, "Designing Organizations for an Information-Rich World," in *Computers, Communications, and the Public Interest*, ed. Martin Greenberger (Baltimore, MD: Johns Hopkins Press, 1971).

[11]See Angela Duckworth, *Grit: The Power of Passion and Perseverance* (New York: Scribner, 2018), and https://angeladuckworth.com/grit-scale/.

1. *Organic or "spot" mentoring.* "Spot mentoring" is my term for organic connections that happen spontaneously on the campus. They take place when educators plan for margin in their day and make themselves available for spontaneous investments, even if for only a few minutes. As an undergraduate at Oral Roberts University, I remember President Roberts entering the dining hall on a regular basis to enjoy lunch at a table with students. I enjoyed an unplanned lunch with him and asked him all sorts of questions about his walk with God. It was more than fellowship. He made emotional and spiritual deposits in me that I've never forgotten. These can happen on a sidewalk when we stop to pray for a student, in the media center when we pause to ask how their studies are going, or in a residence hall when we stop in for a visit on a weekend afternoon. We must be intentional about our serendipity.

2. *Organized mentoring.* These are planned meetings with an individual student or with a small community of students that happen regularly for the purpose of development. I've done this since 1979, and the students and I have discussed books, taken assessments, studied Scripture, or processed current events to build a healthy worldview in students. The key is for members to agree on expectations yet for meetings to feel organic in nature. Organized and organic are a must for Gen Z. Authenticity is more important than political correctness for most students. One university student put it this way to me: "The only thing worse than being uncool is being unreal." These mentoring communities should last for a set time (one year or one semester) and should determine what the objectives should be and what conduct to expect.

3. *Reverse mentoring.* This is a term we first heard from Jack Welch, CEO of General Electric, thirty years ago. As computers were introduced to the workforce, many of his seasoned veterans felt inept at using them; at the same time, most of the new hires out of college felt at home with them. So, he paired up employees that included both a veteran and a rookie, both of whom would be expected to "mentor" the other in their strength. After swapping stories, the veteran would relay how to succeed at GE. Then the rookie would relay how to capitalize on technology to accelerate the work. This gave dignity to both parties and formed relationships that endured for years. I have benefited from these "reverse mentoring" relationships with young people for decades now.

FIVE EXPERIENCES WE MUST OFFER WHEN MENTORING THE NEXT GENERATION OF EDUCATORS

In response to current practices and needs of students, I suggest we consider five experiences students need to have in order to enable themselves to transition from childhood to adulthood. Call them rites of passage. Since 1979, I've been committed to mentoring emerging leaders, both students and young professionals. I became a father in 1988 and now have two adult children. Over time, I identified the most meaningful experiences to my mentees—the ones that mature Gen Z students and build grit and depth. Collectively, they serve as a sort of rite of passage.[12]

1. Do something scary. There is something invigorating about stepping out of our comfort zones to attempt a risky act that's unfamiliar and even a bit frightening. Our senses are heightened when we feel we are taking a risk. We don't know what we're doing; we have to trust and even rely on one another. Ideally, these initiatives are intentional and well planned for our students, but they should not be scripted. They must include the element of chance. As a mentor, I've taken my mentees to spend the night with people living on the streets. Those students were wide-eyed as we interacted with an entirely different population and slept on trash bags with newspapers as a blanket. A small dose of danger mixed with a large dose of unfamiliar accelerates growth. This is true for students of any age. It matures them.

When my son was twelve, we took a father-and-son trip to another city. We explored some new places, but the scariest part of the four-day trip was when I traded places with him in our car and had him drive it around a parking lot. After I explained the gears and peddles, Jonathan overcame his panic and drove the big automobile. In moments, he was grinning from ear

---

[12]Some material in this section is adapted from Tim Elmore with Andrew McPeak, *Generation Z Unfiltered: Facing Nine Hidden Challenges of the Most Anxious Population* (Atlanta: Poet Gardner, 2019).

to ear. This sparked a remarkable conversation, comparing his fear then to what he'll experience while becoming a man. Adulthood is not for the faint-hearted; it's about responsibility and being drivers, not passengers in life.

Facing fears is a rite of passage for young adults. Doing something that's neither prescribed nor guaranteed unleashes adrenaline and other chemicals that awaken us. Other "feel good" chemicals that come into play with scary experiences include dopamine, endorphins, serotonin, and oxytocin. Part of the reason more teens don't come alive is that we've protected them from high-stakes situations in the name of safety.

2. Meet someone influential. Another challenge for young adults is to have them meet someone they deem significant. Because Gen Z may be less comfortable meeting older professionals face-to-face, the encounter itself may stretch them. On top of that, meeting a significant person invites them to prepare questions to ask and fosters listening skills. These can be famous people, but they don't have to be. The key is they're people the students believe to be important because of what they've accomplished. Often a university experience is the first time a student is on their own to connect with and cultivate a relationship with an older adult without the covering of their parents.

I chose to introduce this experience to my own children before their college years. I participated in a special meeting in Washington, DC, when my daughter, Bethany, was just nine years old. Since I'd be meeting members of Congress, ambassadors, and civic leaders, I wanted her to experience it with me. Encountering noteworthy people can be intimidating, even to adults. It was fun to see her meet these people and interact with them, eventually feeling quite at home.

For the first twenty years of my career, I worked for bestselling author John C. Maxwell. My young kids were fortunate enough to build a relationship with John and his wife, Margaret. Interacting with the Maxwells enabled them to overcome social fears and to see noteworthy people as humans. When it was time for my children to attend college, they pursued relationships with professors and mentors handily. Today my kids are not starstruck with celebrities, and they are comfortable interfacing with people of all ages.

3. Travel someplace different. We all know that travel in itself is an education. Although classrooms are useful learning contexts, leaving the classroom and all that's familiar is better still. Not only does travel push students out of their comfort zones, but it also forces them to understand others, connect with new environments, and problem solve; here they cannot default to their subconscious instincts. Consider this: when we're in familiar situations, we can shift into cruise control. On our home turf, we can become numb to reality; life can be lived on autopilot. But this doesn't occur in a foreign location. Mission trips stir our curiosity, beg us to research, beckon us to learn, and invite us to grow. We think new thoughts in new places. Within an hour of meeting a student, I can usually discern the difference between one who's been exposed to a crosscultural experience and one who has not. My friend Glen Jackson says, "A change of pace plus a change of place equals a change of perspective."

One of my favorite memories was taking my five-year-old daughter, Bethany, to Croatia during the Serbian-Bosnian War in 1993. My goal was to enable her to be comfortable in environments that were both foreign and struggling. Bethany helped serve food, offer clothes, and distribute blankets to refugees who had relocated to the area. She saw poverty she'd never seen before and experienced the joy of providing for the needs of those who were displaced and suffering. The experience matured her. By the time she graduated college, she'd been on six such trips.

4. Chase a meaningful goal. I believe students need us to let them pursue an objective that has high stakes and gives them full control. Past generations matured more rapidly because they were given responsibility for jobs and goals that had genuine meaning at a young age. When we lower the stakes or give teens an artificial purpose to engage in, they end up with artificial maturity. Although I believe in the value of academics, it's still a facsimile of a meaningful world, created by our current, contemporary structures. Classrooms are not enough. I meet too many students who master the skill of getting a good grade yet struggle to translate those grades into careers, marriage, and a family. Information is meaningful as it becomes application.

When I speak of chasing a big goal, I mean aiming for a target that has deep meaning to your students, one that stretches their capacity and is important. As a teen, my son, Jonathan, told us he wanted to pursue the entertainment industry. So my wife and I decided to let Jonathan step out at sixteen years old. As a homeschooler, he had more freedom with his time. He and his mom moved from Atlanta to Los Angeles for seven months to try his hand at acting. The experience was revealing, as you can imagine. Life in Burbank at an apartment with hundreds of other kid actors revealed the competitive world there. He soon recognized how much influence the storytellers have behind the camera. Returning home, Jonathan was a different person and clearer on his calling. He later earned a degree in screen writing and now writes scripts every week.

5. *Wait and work for something you want.* One of the reasons teens and college students find adulting so challenging today is that they've grown up in a world where almost everything is instant access and on-demand. It can coerce us to expect instant gratification. The opposite of this trait is patience and a strong work ethic. These signal maturity because the person is able to see a goal in his or her mind that is still invisible externally. This is a critical experience for university students.

Consider what's happening in young adults' brains. Teens who envision an outcome before they actually experience it can cause their brains to release dopamine and endorphins, which signal pleasure and rewards. As they experience "learned industriousness" (*I keep working because I know it will pay off*), acetylcholine kicks in. This chemical plays a vital role in learning and memory, and it deepens neuropathways as kids associate rewards with working toward a goal. In our home, our kids paid for half of their first cars, half of their smartphones, or half of a trip they each wanted to take.

When we provide these five experiences, we practice generativity—the art of providing for younger generations to take their place in the world. Additionally, we bridge the gap between us. My favorite outcome from these experiences for me personally came years later. My daughter, Bethany, called me when she was twenty-five years old and living two thousand miles away. When I asked why she had called, she replied, "I guess I just called to say thanks."

I said, "Well, every dad loves to hear that from his children—but what drove you to call now? Did something happen at work today?"

After collecting her thoughts, she said, "I guess I just noticed that I work with a bunch of young professionals like me, but nobody sees the big picture around here. They act lazy, they're on their phones, and I don't see any work ethic. They're not ready to live on their own!" She paused and then concluded, "I guess I just realized that you and Mom did get me ready. And I just wanted to say thanks."

Through tears, I smiled and replied, "Bethany—you just made my year."

7

WHO WILL LEAD US?

A Lifecycle Approach to Academic Mentorship

BECK A. TAYLOR

I am grateful for an opportunity to reflect on the important topic of mentorship in faithful academic settings. Although this volume is chiefly concerned with the theological and practical underpinnings of raising up the next generation of academic leaders, mentorship is critical for all in the academy, regardless of particular callings into classroom teaching and learning, scholarship, institutional and community service, coaching, student affairs, and various areas of academic administration. For Christian higher education to succeed in transforming the lives of students, thereby equipping graduates to transform a broken world, all elements of the academic enterprise must be populated with professionals flourishing in their respective roles. In my estimation, that ideal demands quality and intentional mentorship at all levels.

What does it mean to flourish professionally? I hope all readers can recount seasons in their careers during which they felt well equipped and supported to do their work. Professional flourishing includes a sense of simple professional competency, usually accompanied by an assurance of learning and growth, in which responsibility and influence on organizational success are pointing to new horizons for professional opportunity and enhanced impact. Additionally, flourishing likely includes proximity to colleagues who feel equally equipped and are themselves thriving professionally. In the mix I see mentors—others with more experience and a generous desire to invest in junior colleagues—who are intentionally setting the stage for continued growth and development for all.

Embedded or implied within this healthy ecosystem is the reality of professional life cycles. In almost all organizations, junior (and often younger) colleagues begin their careers in environments for which they are well trained but uncertain how to succeed. These junior colleagues may have questions about models for success, benchmarks for development, and where to set their sights for future opportunity and growth. Success or failure often depends on how well younger employees are able to articulate their needs and advocate for their success.

Most organizations also include midcareer individuals who successfully navigated the advent of their professional journey but are still in need of career coaching, modeling, and counsel. In my experience, this stage of the professional life cycle is often when people discern their potential calling into leadership; they make important decisions about alternative professional trajectories that can have significant impact on future opportunities. These midcareer individuals, by virtue of their success, have a role to play in the mentoring of junior colleagues. But they are also well served to seek out mentors to help chart their next professional chapter.

Finally, seasoned and senior colleagues who successfully made it to the last stage of their professional careers are often most qualified and most keen to provide the important advice and mentoring needed by those at earlier stages of the life cycle. These sages not only pour into colleagues facing long professional runways, but often benefit from the renewed energy and fresh perspectives of their mentees, thereby adding to their own well-being and sense of flourishing. Ending a career well can be achieved, in part, by investing in the future of the organization and the people who will determine whether that future is successful.

Within the academy, these three stages of the professional life cycle (entry, midcareer, and senior) are strikingly apparent and map well onto traditional faculty ranks.[1] Junior or assistant professors with freshly

---

[1]See Robert Boice, *The New Faculty Member* (San Francisco: Jossey-Bass, 1992); Gary M. Burge, *Mapping Your Academic Career: Charting the Course of a Professor's Life* (Downers Grove, IL: IVP Academic, 2015); Angela Provitera McGlynn, *Successful Beginnings for College Teaching* (Madison,

minted terminal degrees are often thrown into the classroom for the first time with little guidance. Few graduate programs give students real pedagogical education and experience, and new professors are often writing their first course syllabi, thinking for the first time about learning outcomes, assessment, classroom management, integrating faith and learning, accessing university teaching resources, learning campus culture, and starting sustainable research programs.

Even when those challenges are met, new faculty are also too often grasping for an understanding about expectations for service roles at the institution and how much time to spend signaling their support for institutional committee work. All of these challenges occur as assistant professors are trying to understand what they will need to accomplish to contend for tenure and promotion. No wonder junior faculty often, even if quietly, express confusion and anxiety about the process. They desperately need mentors who can help them succeed and flourish.

But what happens after faculty members successfully achieve tenure and are promoted, say, to associate professor and enter the middle years of their careers? Relief over avoiding the pitfalls resulting in an unsuccessful bid for tenure now aside, they face new challenges and uncertainties that require thoughtful attention. What do post-tenure research programs look like, and how do midcareer professors manage the graduate students entrusted into their care? Can they find opportunities to become more creative in the classroom? Are there service areas at the university that need attention and match their interests? Do some leadership roles sound appealing? In addition, what continued trajectory of professional development is required to be promoted to full professor?

My experience indicates that ten to fifteen years into their respective careers, some faculty members stagnate and languish. The annals of higher education are filled with bright and capable colleagues whose promising rise to the rank of associate professor was followed by less-than-stellar achievements that ended in the lack of continued promotion. What

---

WI: Atwood, 2001); and Nancy Archer Martin and Jennifer L. Bloom, *Career Aspirations and Expeditions: Advancing Your Career in Higher Education Administration* (Champaign, IL: Stipes, 2003).

happened? Again, the need for real mentorship is necessary for those in the middle years of their academic careers. In addition, these colleagues are often the most proximate to the junior faculty members coming up the line behind them. Some are asking how best to serve as mentors while also seeking guidance from more senior colleagues.

Finally, although professional productivity can and should continue to characterize faculty members whose record rewards them with full professorship, as I argued, these colleagues are in the best position to carry the load when it comes to mentoring. They are in the best position—in terms of acquired knowledge and wisdom, political power and savvy, and with respect to how they choose to spend their time—to seek out junior and midcareer colleagues to offer their much-needed support. In this career stage, potentially great satisfaction exists in knowing they can contribute to the success of another colleague.

What resources are needed for successful mentorship? Is it an organic process that happens on its own? Or are there guided steps and well-tested programs that can increase the likelihood of a successful mentorship collaboration? Are generous senior colleagues well supported in their desires to pour into the lives of others, or are they left to their own devices?

Although my description of professional life cycles in the academy focused thus far on teaching faculty, these same stages are also evident in the careers of colleagues who serve in other parts of the university. As people move from being staffers to assistant and associate directors, even as they attain titles such as director, assistant or associate vice president, and divisional vice president, the same career life cycle influences the future success of colleagues called to support students and faculty, keep critical systems functional, train and coach athletes, minister to the campus, raise support, and steward financial and capital resources. Flourishing at all levels and in all corners of career service is our desire as we think about a healthy university.

Finally, as it relates to leadership, how are the stages of career progression, the successes at each stage that lead to subsequent promotion, and the impact of mentorship needed to develop employees whose careers in the Christian academy will offer explicit opportunities to lead centers, departments, divisions, and universities influenced by those of us who care deeply about those who will lead us into the future? Although I would argue many kinds of leaders exist on a Christian college campus, how do we identify those colleagues whose experiences and skills uniquely suit critical roles as department chairs, deans, directors, vice presidents, and presidents?

MY PERSONAL JOURNEY WITH LIFECYCLE MENTORSHIP

Undergraduate preparation. Perhaps like so many called to teach in colleges and universities, my story begins at the intersection of a love and aptitude for my chosen discipline of study and formative experiences as an undergraduate that eventually led me to graduate school. I attended Baylor University in Waco, Texas, as an undergraduate, and there I found my first academic mentoring relationships. Although the academic life cycle introduced above started with an initial appointment to a teaching faculty, many academics and those working at universities have stories that begin with mentorship during college.

My undergraduate story features several professors who had a profound impact on my life. Steve Green and Allen Seward, most notable among many others I could name, not only nurtured my growing fascination with economics, but they also modeled an attractive life of learning and faith. They did so by meeting with me during office hours, inviting me into their homes, and accommodating the questions I posed about the benefits and costs of pursing graduate study and an eventual career in the professoriate. My mentors also encouraged me. They explicitly named the strengths they saw in my academic ability and challenged me to consider further education even as they clearly articulated the costs of that decision in terms of time and forgone economic reward. They also modeled Christian humility, charity, and benevolence as they groomed me to pursue a PhD at Purdue University.

There is great value in programs that identify talented undergraduates who may have a future in higher education. As I mention later, students do not necessarily have to head to graduate school to prepare for academic positions; many will be called to other roles around the university. In my experience, few universities have formal affinity groups and clubs that point students to careers in higher education. As was the case for me, most mentoring occurs in smaller settings as faculty members and other university staffers counsel undergrads to think about future careers in the academy. Regardless, the seeds of calling into the Christian university are often planted when students are in college.

Graduate mentorship. Once I arrived in West Lafayette, Indiana, at Purdue University, I was fortunate to find two professors who had room to take me on as a graduate student and who were faithful Christians. I did not seek out fellow believers as my mentors, but God led me to them. Jack Barron and John Umbeck took me under their wings and guided me through a rigorous curriculum and research program that ultimately led to the successful defense of my doctoral dissertation. Many people successfully navigate the challenges of graduate work, but, as Christians, these two men encouraged me in ways that appealed to my calling as a follower of Christ and helped to prepare me for a career at a Christian institution.

To help me with the discernment process, Jack and John asked questions about how I was balancing my graduate studies and my roles as a husband and new father. They talked with me about my desire to return to a Christian university and the potential tradeoffs, depending on the institution I selected. We attended the same church, and I often found myself in John's home, working on projects and talking about life. As with many good graduate advisers, they also fought for me as I applied for faculty openings across the country. Importantly, during my years at Purdue, I remained in close contact with Steve Green and Allen Seward back at Baylor. We spoke and emailed often about my emerging interests. They continued to encourage me, even when I encountered seasons in graduate school when I questioned what I was doing.

Perhaps the kind of Christian mentorship I experienced as a graduate student is more common at Christian doctoral universities; I suspect it is rare at large state universities. Many secular universities have organizations for Christian faculty to share their stories and faith. I know that John Umbeck regularly talked about his Christian journey in such settings at

Purdue.[2] My hope is that in such settings, Christian mentors are intentionally talking to doctoral candidates about possible careers in the Christian academy. This kind of directed talent acquisition will serve our sector well as our institutions compete for qualified junior faculty members.

I recount these stories of early mentorship to underscore the incredible impact Christian faculty mentors have on the lives of their students. The grooming of future academic leaders starts in the undergraduate classroom and continues as talented and motivated students accumulate the credentials for successful reentry as professionals back to the university. I am confident this pattern holds true for our colleagues who serve in areas adjacent to the academic mission. Coaches and athletic directors can point to mentors who nurtured natural athletic and leadership ability into clear vocational callings. Student life professionals often recount spiritual life coordinators, residence hall supervisors, directors of Greek life, and even campus disciplinarians as people who made a real difference in their educational journeys, a difference that ultimately led them to pursue similar or related careers.

Early faculty career. On the completion of my doctoral work, I returned to Baylor as a tenure-track assistant professor in the same department from which I had graduated only five years earlier. Although many in academic leadership today can recount stories similar to the one I have discussed thus far, this point is likely where my journey becomes unique. Fewer people obtain their first academic appointment in their home undergraduate department. I was only the second tenure-track hire in economics at Baylor in ten years. I was only five years removed from my bachelor's degree, and the composition of the economics department was almost identical to the one I left, with the exception of another junior colleague, Mahamudu Bawumia, who arrived a year before me.

At the time, Baylor was just embarking on its ambitious Baylor 2012 strategic plan led by Robert Sloan.[3] That vision called for Baylor to

---

[2]"Prof Talk: John Umbeck," Ratio Christi, video, 9:01, September 12, 2015, https://youtu
.be/6gFStiqpwjQ.
[3]See https://baylor2012.web.baylor.edu; Barry G. Hankins and Donald D. Schmeltekopf, eds., *The Baylor Project* (South Bend, IN: St. Augustine's Press, 2007).

become a more research-intensive university. Because my colleague Mahamudu and I were soon standing for tenure in a department that had not reviewed a tenure case in many years, the economics department began a process of articulating revised standards for tenure and promotion. To my surprise, my more senior colleagues invited Mahamudu and me into the conversations and deliberations that eventually led to the new standards.

Although the suggestion may seem potentially unorthodox, I believe junior colleagues who are asked to meet certain thresholds of teaching proficiency and scholarly production to reach tenure and promotion should be asked occasionally to reflect on how they perceive those standards. Are they in line with contemporary expectations? How do they compare with standards at other similar universities? Are they appropriately rigorous? Do they accurately assess the quality of teaching and scholarship? Seeking that kind of input might serve departments well as they mentor junior faculty through the tenure and promotion process.

During my years as an untenured faculty member at Baylor, I benefited from the same quality mentorship I experienced as an undergraduate. The department hired two more junior colleagues, Chuck North and Tisha Emerson, in successive years. Before too long, a whole cadre of newer colleagues populated the department, all at similar stages in our careers. My sense is that my junior colleagues and I had ready access to department members eager to answer questions about professional development, to collaborate on teaching and research initiatives, and to acquire resources for data, travel, course releases, and all of the many inputs needed to fuel the careers of junior faculty. Just as important, my senior mentors were also intentional in helping us center our demanding teaching and research expectations within our callings as Christ followers who worked at a Christian university. Meetings always opened in prayer, and departmental brown-bag lunches were devoted to topics such as faith-learning integration, teaching excellence, research methods, and departmental strategies—strategies largely dependent on the outputs of us junior colleagues.

Our economics department flourished in those years, in part because of the increased resources provided by the Baylor 2012 plan, which led to even more hiring at the junior (Carl Gwin) and senior (Earl Grinols and David VanHoose) levels, but also because of the creative, empowering culture our senior colleagues (led by then–department chair Steve Green, my former undergraduate adviser) created for their junior colleagues. With the exception of Mahamudu—who, shortly after I arrived, headed back to his home country of Ghana to pursue a career in policy and politics (he is now the vice president of Ghana)—all of us in that early group of new hires at Baylor received tenure and promotion. I benefited from an appointment to a newly endowed professorship.

On the academic side of the university, tenure and promotion are the most important rungs of professional development for future leaders. This part of my story highlights the importance of supporting junior colleagues with access, resources, and mentoring. Similarly, junior colleagues in student affairs, business affairs, athletics, and development require supportive environments to grow and develop. Moving from new employee with novice status to more senior ranks is the first signal of career success, and efforts to set new employees up for achievement must be made to ensure a steady stream of talent is being cultivated for future leadership.

Administrative calling. Other authors would expound at this point about the importance of support they received in the midcareer stage of the academic life cycle. Doing so is harder for me because of the particular shape of my career trajectory. My time as an untenured junior faculty member lasted only three years. After an unusually fortunate and successful run as an assistant professor at Baylor, I was tenured and promoted to an endowed chair at the age of thirty. I did not experience the typical lifecycle progression through the rank of associate professor. For reasons I will explain shortly, I all but skipped this developmental stage.

Nevertheless, I contend that this "sandwich" stage of the academic life cycle presents unique challenges and opportunities to those who successfully garnered tenure but whose careers are far from complete. Colleagues in midcareer roles often find themselves called upon to mentor individuals still in the early years of their careers while seeking out continued mentorship for the all-important ascent to full professor. Although many universities have formal mentoring programs for junior faculty, in my experience universities are less intentional about the next stage of professional development. As previously noted, tenured associate professors can languish for years unless clear expectations for promotion are articulated and unless they are mentored for success. Effective post-tenure evaluation policies for associate professors are scarce, and many of our academic colleagues retire at that rank.

My journey proceeded differently than most. After a one-year sabbatical at Harvard University as a visiting scholar (another resource heaped on me by my supportive colleagues at Baylor), I was invited to participate in a new and innovative program called the Baylor Leadership Challenge. Led by Marilyn Crone, then Baylor's vice president for enrollment and retention, the Baylor Leadership Challenge was formed as a talent identification and cultivation initiative designed to raise up the next generation of institutional leaders at Baylor.

The first year of the program was populated with about a dozen faculty and staff members from across the university, each distinguished in some way that caused senior leaders to want to expose them to leadership mentoring and experiences. A wonderfully successful program, participants gathered for a full day once a month to learn about an area of the university such as athletics, enrollment, and finance. We were also introduced to leaders who gave oversight to those areas. We were then confronted with real challenges these areas were facing and asked to brainstorm solutions. In the midst of these far-ranging conversations, I was able to test leadership ideas, read what others wrote, be exposed to current leaders and hear their perspectives, and gain direct access to Baylor's most senior leaders.

This last point served as a meaningful inflection point in my own career. As part of the Baylor Leadership Challenge program, each participant was paired with a university leader-mentor for the entire year. I was paired with Baylor's president, Robert Sloan. During the year, I shadowed Robert, attended meetings with him, met one-on-one to discuss university issues, and asked for career advice. As was the case with my previous professional mentors, Robert was generous with his time, sincerely interested in my well-being, and eager to help me discern whether academic leadership was in my future. We read books and articles together, and I felt as though I had unfettered access, something I tried not to abuse. However, I can remember copious hours alongside Robert as he thought through and prayed about issues he faced. Although it was a difficult year for Robert (he stepped down just a year later), I decided during that season to pursue leadership, a decision that eventually led me to a presidency.

Formal leadership development programs such as the one at Baylor yield obvious benefits for individuals who participate and for the institution itself. Universities spot and cultivate future leaders. Individuals who are tapped feel empowered and equipped to continue their leadership development. Risks, however, also exist. Many faith-based universities are relatively flat in their organizational design, meaning not many layers of leadership exist. The number of vice presidencies, directorships, and deanships at smaller universities is limited.

Once colleagues complete such a program, they may begin looking for a place within the organization to move and exert greater leadership and responsibility. Unfortunately, because of size and timing issues, those opportunities do not always exist, and colleagues can feel disheartened. I have seen colleagues leave the university not long after completing such a course because few opportunities for upward mobility at their institution existed. Although we can celebrate when Christian higher education gets stronger as a sector due to intentional professional development, losing valued employees may be hard—especially those in whom a lot of investment was made.

My path to the presidency. After completing my one-year mentorship with Robert Sloan in the Baylor Leadership Challenge, my dean at the Hankamer School of Business, Terry Maness, created a new associate deanship to support research and faculty development and graciously named me to be its first occupant. Terry's decision to entrust me with this new strategic position was a function of the ways that Baylor and the Hankamer School of Business, from the time I was an undergraduate, invested in my career and success. (Perhaps it is also not surprising to know that Terry was himself another important undergraduate mentor of mine.)

My time in that new role, however, was short. After only a year, and because of the countless ways mentors had invested in my life to that point, Samford University, in Birmingham, Alabama, recruited me to become dean of its business school. At age thirty-five, I was the youngest dean of a business school accredited by the prestigious Association to Advance Collegiate Schools of Business. What drew me to Samford was once again an opportunity to be mentored, this time by legendary Baptist leader and Samford's longtime president, Tom Corts.

Knowing of Tom's outsized leadership role in Christian higher education, I eagerly accepted the call to work with him. Samford was a growing and comprehensive university, but one with an underperforming business school. I was ready for the challenge of cultivating the school's potential. With Tom, I had the motivation I needed to move away from my alma mater. Sadly for me, only five months later, Tom announced his retirement from Samford. God was faithful again, however, and Andy Westmoreland, after a successful season as president of Ouachita Baptist University in Arkadelphia, Arkansas, succeeded Tom as president.

My time learning from Andy Westmoreland was enormously valuable. We worked together regularly to raise funds and excitement for Samford's growing business programs. He was incredibly generous with his time, and we spent hours together in his office, in his home, and on the road talking about the future of Samford and Christian higher education. Not long after his arrival, Andy developed an informal group of Samford colleagues, all up-and-comers, and nicknamed it the future presidents club. Often with Andy in attendance, and also independently with one another, this group met regularly to talk, learn, pray, and discern what God was calling Samford to be, and how each of us could play a role. In addition to myself, that group included Joe Hopkins, now president at Campbellsville University, and Chuck Sands, now provost at California Baptist University and no doubt on a presidential trajectory. Others in the group are now presidents of K-12 Christian academies and associate deans of leading theological schools.

Andy Westmoreland's prescient formation of a mentoring cadre speaks volumes of his commitment to nurturing future leadership and preparing

Samford and the Christian academy for success. Informal programs, such as our future presidents club, and formal ones, such as the Baylor Leadership Challenge, equip and empower future leaders to gain access to experiences and resources that serve them and their institutions well into the future. Again, the risk always exists of setting expectations high for colleagues who want to pursue leadership roles at the institution, and sometimes employees will leave for bigger opportunities. That was my story.

After five years at Samford and four years working with Andy, the time came for my own presidency. Whitworth University in Spokane, Washington, called me in 2010 to become its eighteenth president, following the very successful presidency of Bill Robinson. Although nothing can fully prepare one for the college presidency, the experiences mentors offered me made my ascendency to the presidency one that made sense. I now understood most parts of the modern university. I was grounded in success as a faculty member, as a junior administrator, and as an academic dean. I benefited from being mentored by three sitting presidents. Andy and Bill continued to mentor and guide me as I grew into my role as president at Whitworth.

Finally, after a successful eleven-year presidency at Whitworth, life came full circle once again. In 2021, Samford appointed me its nineteenth president, succeeding my good friend and mentor, Andy Westmoreland. A presidency at an institution I already knew and loved was simply too good to pass up, especially one where I could continue to access the wisdom and insights of the former president and my longtime mentor.

My personal story is not likely replicated with any frequency, and doing so may not be ideal. For instance, I am sure I made plenty of mistakes early in my leadership because I was promoted so quickly into administrative roles. My journey, however, highlights the benefits of academic mentorship as I moved from undergraduate to graduate student, and then from assistant professor to academic dean, and eventually into institutional leadership. At every step of the way, senior colleagues and mentors guided my journey and ensured I was prepared for future opportunities. I benefited from formal mentorship and professional development programs as well as from informal relationships with mentors who were generous with time and advice.

As a postscript to my autobiographical journey of mentorship and leadership, another group of mentor-like peers merits recognition. At the beginning of my Whitworth presidency, several other Christian college and university leaders and I formed an informal group that began meeting at the Broadmoor in Colorado Springs once a year to encourage one another and share ideas about how to make the incredibly demanding presidential role more sustainable for healthy spiritual lives and marriages. That group of nine other Christian university presidents and their spouses is an incredible source of support and inspiration for my wife, Julie, and me. Navigating nearly twelve years in presidential roles is hard to imagine without those colleagues. They form a network of peers, certainly, but many elements found in good mentorship are evident in our group's relational dynamics.

IDENTIFYING FUTURE LEADERS

As we guide our colleagues along their own lifecycle journeys, how can we be intentional about identifying future leaders and investing in their professional development? What characteristics should we be looking for in individuals we mentor?

The personal journey I described was replete with examples of how mentors benefited my own professional development. At each stage, I also had many opportunities to mentor others. As a tenured professor, I regularly spoke with junior colleagues about their own professional aspirations. When possible, I included them in research projects and led conversations about excellent teaching. Because I invested in Christian higher education for most of my career, I gave considerable thought to the role of Christ-centered higher education and our goals to integrate Christian faith and learning. I have always tried to lead junior faculty in their own explorations of that topic.

As a dean, I had many opportunities not only to invest time in my faculty and other administrators, but also to support programs designed for their professional development. As an academic administrator, I had responsibility for budgets and other resources designated to assist faculty members and junior administrators with their own professional needs. I was able to send faculty members to conferences, support grant proposals, and talk with administrators about the next steps in their leadership portfolio. Many of the former faculty members I served as a dean now fill important leadership roles, including as department chairs, deans, and even university presidents.

Finally, as a president I often speak with faculty members and administrators about their professional aspirations. I give leadership to institution-wide efforts to improve teaching, research, and grant writing. Many nonacademic staff members eagerly discuss how they can grow in professional responsibility. I support workshops, programs, and outside speakers, all meant to encourage university employees and their unique professional needs. Additionally, I serve as the direct supervisor for a cadre of vice presidents and senior administrators, many with professional aspirations. Importantly, I also give voice to broader issues that impact Christian higher education. One of my most important roles as president is appointing leaders throughout the organization.

In my experience, I associate several characteristics and strengths with leadership potential within Christian higher education, regardless of the employee's stage of professional development or area of service. Future leaders are often quite diverse in their backgrounds, experiences, and skill sets, and that diversity serves institutions well. Regardless, most successful leaders possess certain strengths of particular importance. Of course, we want leaders who are honest, live with integrity, display kindness and compassion, and make good moral choices. Beyond those nonnegotiable virtues, mentors should focus on identifying and helping to amplify this select group of characteristics among their mentees.

Mission orientation. For institutions of higher education that confess the lordship of Jesus Christ, the most important characteristic of future leaders, regardless of their stage of professional development, is their identification with and support of the university's mission. Irrespective of the institution's particular theological or denominational tradition, faculty and administrative leaders must see their institution's faithful convictions as central to the organization's ability to deliver on its mission.[4]

---

[4]Caroline J. Simon, ed., *Mentoring for Mission* (Grand Rapids, MI: Eerdmans, 2003).

Hiring with this characteristic in mind is crucial for success; what's more, giving employees opportunities to explore topics such as vocation, faith-learning integration, and Christian leadership will enable them to grow in their connection to and appreciation for their institution's mission. The most effective Christian universities, in my opinion, are ones that provide plenty of forums for faculty and staff members to think well about the institution's Christian identity.[5]

In my own experience, I benefited while serving at Baylor in and through departmental and university-wide conversations that invited me to think about my vocation as a Christian professor and the university's faithful identity. Nearly all speeches or remarks I give as a university president reflect on the university's mission and ways to strengthen it. In particular, I strive to ensure that programs and spaces are devoted to such conversations and rising leaders encounter opportunities to reflect on their own identities and commitments that strengthen the university's overall mission.

Service to others. By definition, leadership involves serving others. Even early in a faculty or staff member's career, one can often spot a generous spirit, an eagerness to contribute to the community, and an outward orientation. The demands on junior faculty members are enormous. The road to tenure and promotion demands self-discipline and a work ethic attentive to individual goals and output. Shielding junior faculty colleagues from onerous service commitments is important. On the other hand, a colleague who demonstrates no desire to meet service commitments and whose demeanor does not reflect a desire to serve things greater than themselves is not a likely a candidate for leadership development.

My own career benefited from senior colleagues who modeled a service orientation that sought to strengthen their institution and contribute to

---

[5]Douglas V. Henry and Michael D. Beaty, eds., *Christianity and the Soul of the University* (Grand Rapids, MI: Baker Academic, 2006); Arthur F. Holmes, *Building the Christian Academy* (Grand Rapids, MI: Eerdmans, 2001); Mark A. Noll, *The Scandal of the Evangelical Mind* (Grand Rapids, MI: Eerdmans, 1994); Robert Benne, *Quality with Soul* (Grand Rapids, MI: Eerdmans, 2001); David S. Dockery, ed., *Faith and Learning* (Nashville: B&H Academic, 2012); and David S. Dockery and David P. Gushee, *The Future of Christian Higher Education* (Nashville: B&H Academic, 1999).

their colleagues' flourishing. Early in my career at Baylor, I helped draft important departmental policies, serve on curriculum committees, and give important input into institutional strategy. Those opportunities gave me the ability to see a bigger picture, form meaningful relationships with senior colleagues, and exercise newfound leadership abilities. I am sure many of the subsequent opportunities I was given in my career were influenced, in part, by others seeing in me a desire to contribute to the whole.

Professional intentionality. I have read plenty of stories about "accidental" leaders—people who stumbled into their leadership roles with little forethought or intentional effort. Those stories are the exception and not the rule, in my experience. Intentionality about professional growth and opportunity is a common characteristic of future leaders. Leaders want to make progress. They want to learn new things and have enriching experiences. People with this orientation seek me out for conversations about what is next. Those conversations keep me on my toes as I am then required to help plan and develop opportunities for motivated employees.

People with this orientation often ask about what I am reading, whether I noticed a particular news story, or how I am considering an important institutional decision. They often seek out formal mentoring relationships and watch leaders, gleaning helpful habits and practices that contribute to their own professional development. Employees concerned about their professional development and trajectory often stand to benefit most greatly from our mentoring efforts.

As I reflect on my own professional journey, my intentional efforts to grow and develop, first as a faculty member and then as an academic administrator, were surely useful as I navigated the steps needed to move into larger roles and take on more administrative responsibility. I was eager to read, attend conferences, and shadow leaders in my life so I could learn more and make wiser decisions about how to allocate my time and effort. Closely observing the habits and practices of individuals I emulated was important to me, and I would often ask my mentors to share their best practices with me. As a leader, I am now quick to notice these patterns in employees who have interests in leadership, and I attempt to share as generously with them as my mentors have with me.

Work ethic. Work-life balance is important. We want employees who flourish, and part of that flourishing requires healthy boundaries, ones that protect physical and mental health, family and friends, and avocational interests. Most successful leaders also have extra reservoirs of energy, time, and productivity. Making commitments and meeting them, delivering on projects with timeliness and quality, volunteering for important roles, and a willingness to stand in the gap when things are not proceeding in a timely or effective way are all signals to consider. As the demands on leaders expand and become more complex, the ability to navigate them will require an ample supply of commitment to the work, and an ability to juggle in healthy ways the many demands of life and career.

When exploring leadership with potential mentees, I often ask questions about their work habits and other priorities in their lives. It is important for me to learn about their interests outside of work and how they manage time. Most often, employees with healthy work habits will distinguish themselves with a high level of professional output. I also watch for individuals who experience meaningful lives outside of work.

Openness to mentorship. Finally, one of the most sincere and endearing traits among future leaders is their willingness and desire to be mentored. I initiated many of my own experiences with being mentored by asking some version of "Will you be my mentor?" When colleagues come to me with that question or somehow indicate they are eager to learn from me, I make an effort to serve them. Those colleagues who seek out mentorship are often humble, teachable, and ready to learn. Seeking a formal mentoring relationship is also a sign of the professional intentionality, mentioned earlier.[6]

CONCLUSION

The opportunity to contribute to the success of another person is one of the most fulfilling and rewarding of human experiences. My own professional journey is highlighted with examples of selfless colleagues who spent time and energy ensuring I was equipped and ready for the professional goals and aspirations I formed for myself. In turn, I devoted my

---

[6]James M. Houston, *The Mentored Life: From Individualism to Personhood* (Colorado Springs: Nav-Press, 2002).

professional career to giving back to individuals in my charge in ways that enable, empower, and encourage other employees who are eager to learn and grow into leadership roles.

Recognizing that careers in Christian higher education are often characterized by natural and often discernible professional lifecycle stages can influence how we think about identifying and coming alongside colleagues who will provide future leadership. Employees in our academic and administrative ranks who display uncommon commitments to institutional mission, professional development, and service to others, and who pair those characteristics with a strong work ethic and a willingness to be mentored, are ones for whom we should exercise particular care and concern.

CONCLUSION

A Season of Promise?

STACY A. HAMMONS

We began our exploration of mentoring, the academic vocation, and Christian higher education by asking whether we are experiencing a season of promise or peril. Do the characteristics purported to exist among Millennials and Gen Z, for example, bode well or ominously for Christian education as younger generations enter the academy? What can we be doing now to disciple young academicians in their faith and mentor them into their vocations and the expectations of higher education? How can colleges and universities be prepared to socialize young faculty, including those of color and females, for thriving in their career roles? At the same time, how can seasoned institutional members learn from these new community members in ways that improve Christian universities for all faculty, staff, administrators, and students? How can Christian theology inform new mentorship philosophies and programs, as well as invite critical reflection on those already in existence?

This conclusion strives to answer these questions, at least in part, by first summarizing the findings and arguments found within previous chapters as to the challenges involved in creating a theologically based mentorship program for younger generations and the benefits argued to result by investing in such. Building on the lessons learned, this concluding chapter will offer several propositions for educators to consider as they design or redesign their own mentorship programs. Despite the possible perils and pitfalls, this volume argues that the future of Christian higher education be viewed as one of promise, as new generations of Christian academicians are more firmly grounded, through theologically informed mentorship, in their faith, their vocation, and the mission of Christian higher education.

LESSONS LEARNED

Challenge of theological bases for mentoring. A foundational challenge to the development of theologically informed mentorship is the lack of theological sophistication among evangelical Christians. As described by Clydesdale in chapter two, young evangelical Christians too often lack vocational reflection. They tend to err in one of two directions. More commonly, they make their choices based on cultural practices and values, justifying those choices with religious terminology. Alternatively, though less commonly, they may minimize or even fail to recognize the call of God on the vocational choices they made. Absent in both of these alternatives, according to Clydesdale, are notions of discernment and summoning. Discernment, as discussed in chapter two, involves both internal and external processes to help one reflect on God's gifting. Summoning entails obedience to God's call on one to engage in work needing to be done.

A concomitant challenge is the tendency to overlook the need for any theological basis to mentorship and jump immediately to the nuts and bolts of a mentorship program itself. But, as Colón-Emeric maintains in chapter four, the first consideration in the creation of any mentoring should be teleological; that is, asking, What is the purpose of mentorship? The answer offered by Colón-Emeric is the creation of a new *we* that recognizes the diversity within the Christian academy as well as within God's kingdom. To create this *we,* a diverse array of mentors and mentees must engage in a shared journey of theological and prayerful reflection, the end result being a new sense of belonging and solidarity. A part of this journey involves rejecting fear as a response to difference and embracing reconciliation. An additional aspect of the journey recognizes the need for historically disenfranchised groups to grieve their exclusion. Such grief processes build on scriptural practices of lament, particularly from the Old Testament, and are critical if genuine reconciliation is to occur and if an inclusive *we* is to be created through mentorship.

Challenge of the role of the organization. A second set of challenges concerns the role of higher education institutions themselves in the mentorship process. As Diddams argues in chapter three, vocational calling is typically interpreted as an individual endeavor, the emphasis being on finding one's personal sense of purpose. Missing from the discussion is the role of the organization in (1) structuring and shaping the relationships between its members and (2) creating the context in which one will live out one's vocational calling. To address this oversight, many faculty mentorship programs provide new faculty with information about successfully navigating the organization and simultaneously address new faculty members' concerns. Although certainly helpful, this approach to faculty mentorship misses the opportunity for the organization to learn from its new members, asking, How can the organization change and adapt to better carry out its mission and fulfill its purpose? Instead, the focus remains solely on the individual.

Additionally, an organization's administrative structure, curricular design, co-curricular arrangements, and policies and procedures can either (1) invite new faculty into total membership and involvement in living out the organization's mission or (2) relegate some faculty to no better than the status of perennial guest. Faculty who remain in this latter category for too long can experience disengagement and indifference. Such exclusion may result from explicit or implicit racialized and gendered policies and practices within the organization (see below for a further discussion of this particular topic) or from differential expectations of the generations with regard to the characteristics of a healthy, functioning workplace.

Taylor reminds us that our younger colleagues as well as our midcareer colleagues benefit from mentoring. Such efforts are especially important when considering the cultivation of the next generation of leaders. Colleges and universities that look to cultivate leaders at the time of their appointment to leadership positions have done so too late. Taylor helps us appreciate that mentoring for leadership is incremental, that it happens over time, and that colleges and universities need to offer their younger and midcareer colleagues opportunities to participate in leadership succession programs. Some of those individuals may take leadership positions at other institutions. As Taylor contends, that risk is a worthwhile price for making sure the next generation is prepared to lead.

As Hong argues in chapter five, Millennials and Gen Z employees are more prepared than their predecessors to leave workplaces that have not adapted to their needs and desires with regard to work and a work community. Mentorship programs that do not address structural impediments to the flourishing of all their faculty will flounder in their attempts to help new academicians embrace their vocational calling and be grounded in and committed to their institution's mission.

Challenge of considerations for Millennials and Gen Z entering the academy. A third set of challenges to effective mentorship is offered in chapters one, five, and six. Herein, the authors discuss critical ways in which Millennials and Gen Zers are different from the workforce generations proceeding them. One fundamental difference concerns the use of technology. As discussed by Hong, Millennials have been immersed in technology their entire lives. As a result, they challenge traditional notions of the workplace that expect employees, including faculty, to be physically present for many of the activities involved in the work role. These younger generations desire greater flexibility in how they enact their faculty life and in how they balance their various personal and professional commitments. These views may be in contrast to those held by older colleagues, often called on to be mentors, and in contrast to the working assumptions of the university instituting the mentoring program.

Elmore, in chapter six, expands on Hong's thesis to argue that several factors, including technology, are responsible for both the widening and the acceleration of the "generation gap." Differential exposure not only to technology, but also to changes such as increased mobility and life expectancy (to name only a few), produced different generational life perspectives, impacting approaches to a host of issues, including vocation and employment. The rapidity of these changes is widening the gap between older and younger generations. Again, those changes can create challenges between mentors and mentees, who are typically at least one generation apart if not more.

An additional challenge includes a reduced role of older individuals in the lives of young adults, even as the young report less trust in peers to provide useful advice and guidance. Rather, as Kinnaman maintains in chapter one, we currently inhabit a "digital Babylon," where Millennials and Gen Zers are mentored by Google and social media even while, according to Elmore, they express a preference for face-to-face interaction. At a time when these younger generations may most need the wisdom of more mature individuals to help them grapple with such issues as the pressure to be successful, the imposter syndrome, and existential questions of meaning and purpose, they are less likely to have substantive relationships with older adults who can help them navigate their concerns. Mentoring programs are intended to facilitate such cross-generational relationships, yet, if the mentors and mentees do not work to find commonality, stereotypes and misunderstandings can hamper their relationship and the successfulness of the mentorship.

Challenge of considerations for professionals entering the academy. Yet another set of challenges to the development of theologically informed mentorship concerns the needs of professionals entering the academy. Because these professionals come to higher education with several years of employment experience (in fields such as social work, nursing, physical therapy, business, and education), they are frequently older than young adults and thus are unlikely to be Millennials or Gen Zers. But because they are new to the faculty role, academic vocational mentoring and socialization may prove as critical for them as for young adults. However, these needs may be overlooked due to what Clydesdale labels "generational theorizing." Such theorizing about unique characteristics belonging to distinct birth cohorts can exacerbate differences between generations, overlook the impact of maturation and life course effects, and minimize shared concerns and issues across the different age groups.

The imposter syndrome, discussed by Diddams, is one such issue commonly found among all new employees. In fact, I would argue, this syndrome is as likely to occur (if not more so) among older professionals entering the academy as among Millennials and Gen Zers, because professionals were often successful in their previous careers but now find themselves entering a new role for which they received little guidance or socialization. My institution, Indiana Wesleyan University, hires many working professionals because of our large number of professional programs. To a person, these new faculty members report experiencing a sense of disequilibrium in their self-identity; having left successful careers where they felt and were seen by others as competent, they now find themselves as "newbies" in a very different work environment with different expectations for success. Another example of an issue impacting all employees, not just Millennials and Gen Zers, is burnout (highlighted by Hong in her chapter).

The challenge, then, for any effective theologically informed mentorship program is recognizing the unique issues brought into the academy by Millennials and Gen Zers, while also being aware of shared concerns that new faculty may have across the varied generations. In addition, new faculty members from older generations, say Boomers and Busters (alluded to by Elmore in his chapter), may need unique programming to address birth cohort issues specific to them. Such diversity in approach is required if all new faculty are to thrive in their implementation of the faculty role.

Challenge of diversity. A final set of challenges identified by the authors in this volume concerns diversity. As argued by Colón-Emeric, ethnic diversity, rather than being embraced and celebrated, is too often viewed as a threat by an institution's dominant group. This feeling persists despite demographic evidence pointing to the paucity of racial and ethnic diversity within the academy. Racialized organizational policies and procedures, whether intended or not, prevent faculty of color from becoming authentic and valued members of the community. To succeed in such organizations, faculty of color are required to be the ones engaging in "cultural commutes" from their own historical or cultural group to the organization created and inhabited by the dominant group. Such commutes take a heavy toll on the physical and emotional well-being of these faculty.

Likewise, Hong describes various ways by which the academy enacts gendered policies and practices, exacerbated by the coronavirus pandemic. These challenges include increased work-life balance tensions, the reluctance of employers to adopt flexible and remote work policies, and the subsequent outcome of burnout. While not unique to women, such tensions are experienced at a higher rate by women than by men because women continue to remain more responsible for caregiving and household responsibilities.

Those developing and creating theologically informed mentorship within such racialized and gendered settings must recognize the challenges and issues experienced by women and faculty of color and rely on mentors who likewise grasp or have personally experienced these issues. At the same time, as Diddams reminds us, the focus cannot be solely on helping the individual to adapt. Rather, the mentorship program needs to also address how the organization can be revised so faculty feel appreciated and valued not only for their work contributions, but also for their identities. In addition, Taylor contends such efforts are essential when cultivating leaders.

Organizational benefits. Despite the challenges mentioned in creating theologically informed mentorship within the academy, several benefits have been emphasized. If, for example, such mentorship has engaged its mentors and mentees, as well as the host organization, in a shared journey toward the development of a new sense of *we* as described by Colón-Emeric, a community can be created where genuine reconciliation occurs. Such a community can serve as a powerful example to other Christian organizations and also to secular ones; this is how true reconciliation and healing can take place.

In addition to the creation of a new *we,* other organizational adaptations and improvements can occur when institutions hear the voices of all their employees and change accordingly. As described by Diddams, this reciprocity between an organization and its members helps create a more "vibrant and humane institution." Such institutions become caring communities where all members feel supported and more thoroughly invested in carrying out the institution's mission.

Individual benefits. A benefit of such mentorship to individuals is found in chapters by Hong and Elmore. Mentorship that brings together different generations and helps each generation get past stereotypes of the others can begin to address the issues that Millennials and Gen Zers are experiencing in the academy, including a lack of clarity about their vocational calling; the pressure to be successful; isolation from others; the imposter syndrome; and feelings of depression, loneliness, and insecurity. Additionally, such mentorship can develop inner resourcefulness and resiliency. Likewise, mentorship that recognizes that all new faculty bring issues into the workplace, regardless of their birth cohort, can address those concerns more effectively.

More important, theologically informed mentorship can help individuals address larger issues of faith development and flourishing. As Kinnaman demonstrates, members of Gen Z experience existential concerns regarding life's uncertainty, their relationship to God, and their purpose in life. They lack guidance in knowing what Jesus is calling them to do with their vocations, something that theologically informed mentorship can provide. Likewise, older adults may have some of these same existential concerns and questions. As Clydesdale reminds us,

> Young adults want meaningful lives; so do older adults. Young adults want to make a difference through their work, enjoy companionship with their friends, and find love and tranquility in their homes; so do older adults. And those young adults considering academic vocations want to pursue scholarly projects that are important and valued; so do their older academic mentors. . . . The desire for love, significance, and meaningful work transcends age.

Well-developed theologically informed mentorship can provide guidance to all generations and allow mentors and mentees to learn and grow from deep relationships with one another.

WHERE TO FROM HERE?
PROPOSITIONS FOR EDUCATORS

Although the contributors to this volume identify several challenges to the development of theologically informed mentorship, they also identify how these challenges can be addressed and overcome so as to realize the potential and benefits of such mentorship. This conclusion will now translate that information into propositions for the academy to consider.

PROPOSITION 1: The fundamental basis of the mentorship proposed herein must be rooted in Christian theological principles for the purposes of Christian formation and calling.

Theologically informed relationships existing between mentors and mentees constitute the basis of such mentorship. These relationships move beyond stereotypes of one another's generation and address questions of meaning, purpose, and vocation. Additionally, this type of mentorship provides a venue where issues such as anxiety, loneliness, the pressure to succeed, and exposure to trauma are freely discussed and where vocational and relational discipleship occurs. Reflection and practice allow mentees to grapple with these issues in safety with a trusted mentor, helping to create resiliency. Other critical issues often addressed include feelings of pain and exclusion experienced by faculty of color and women as they attempt to enter and thrive in the academy.

To enable the creation of mentorship based on principles of Christian formation and calling, institutions must reorient their philosophy as to the sort of mentors they need and the preparation those mentors will require to be effective. At one point in time, information about how to successfully navigate the organization and absorb the institution's values, goals, and behavioral expectations may have been sufficient for mentors to know and relay to mentees. But the mentorship proposed here will require much more of mentors. Mentors will need to be theologically educated and able to recognize the working of the Holy Spirit in their own lives in terms of vocational discernment, reflection, and summoning. They must also be willing to make themselves open and vulnerable to their mentees, honestly sharing their own stories of faith and vocational formation. Rather than merely knowing facts, mentors must be prepared to enter into a shared journey with mentees, where both can learn from each other and speak into each other's lives.

PROPOSITION 2: For the theologically informed mentorship proposed in this volume to succeed, the organization must be as willing to change as the mentees.

In her chapter, Diddams describes three models of organizational socialization used to onboard new employees. The earliest model, mentioned earlier in this chapter, focuses on providing information to help new employees acclimate to the expectations and goals of the institution. The second model goes a step further and incorporates the requirements and needs of the new employees into the socialization process. For example, the liminal space inhabited by new employees is addressed and minimized, so one's sense of calling better aligns with the goals and mission of the institution, the new employee is more likely to experience role clarity, and the self-efficacy of the new organizational members is strengthened.

Despite these improvements, this more recent model too is insufficient for the mentorship advocated in this volume. As contributors to this volume detailed, a considerable number of ways exist in which the organization must adapt if it is to meet the needs of new employees *and* more effectively fulfill its mission. So, what is needed is not a static institution, but rather a learning organization that continually transforms itself while also facilitating the learning of its organizational members. The inclusion model presented by Diddams best captures this dual focus. Such a model in higher education would not only seek to address the needs, issues, and concerns new faculty bring into the institution, but also create space and empowerment for those new faculty to have a voice in shaping their work environments.

PROPOSITION 3: Mentorship must recognize and address the needs of Millennials and Gen Zers as they enter the academy.

As detailed by several contributors to this volume, when they enter the academy, Millennials and Gen Zers bring with them not only issues and concerns, but also a different orientation to work and life. If they are to help these younger mentees confront their fears and develop resourcefulness and resiliency, mentors need preparation to discuss these issues with new faculty from these cohorts, moving past any stereotypes they may hold about younger generations. These conversational topics are in addition to the more existential issues already discussed under Proposition 1. Likewise, mentorship needs to help mentees confront their own preconceived notions about older generations such as the Boomers and Busters. Addressing misconceptions about each other is critical if vocational and relational discipleship is to occur between mentor and mentee.

Another aspect of recognizing and addressing the needs of the Millennial and Gen Z cohorts concerns changes the organization itself may need to make to better prepare for increasing presence of members of these generations in the workplace. As suggested by Hong, the workplace needs to reorient itself from a bureaucratic and structured setting to a more "human-centered design" if it is to allow Millennials and Gen Zers to flourish in the academy. Such a workplace, as described by Hong, is characterized by flexibility that allows employees to achieve a better work-life balance. Such considerations are needed, because many of these employees, especially women, are caring for their young children and the needs of their aging parents. Another characteristic of a human-centered design workplace is its intentionality in creating community and connection, qualities strongly desired by Millennials and Gen Zers. Finally, such a workplace values people and treats them as their most valuable asset.

PROPOSITION 4: Mentorship must identify and deal with the needs of professionals entering the academy.

Although not typically Millennials or from Gen Z, professionals leaving careers to enter the academy also face challenges (as described earlier in this chapter). Mentors may need education as to what these challenges are and how best to approach them, given that professionals may be hesitant to admit they are experiencing disequilibrium as a result of entering a new field. Because these mentees may be the same age or generation as their mentors, and because they have had prior professional work experience, both mentors and mentees may make assumptions about how easily the mentees should settle into their new roles. When these assumptions are made, mentors cease to take the time to listen to the actual frustrations that mentees are experiencing. Needed are mentors who can remember their own liminal stress when they first became faculty and thereby help mentees navigate these emotions.

On the organizational level and as Diddams points out, such feelings must be recognized and normalized for all new faculty. Practices such as classroom teaching should be approached from a developmental model rather than an evaluative one so as to help all new faculty learn and grow in their teaching roles. Likewise, the need to feel invested in one's organizational community is not unique to Millennials or Gen Zers. Rather, all employees experience the need to feel a part of the institution even as they do not want to lose their uniqueness in doing so. For such a sense of investment to occur, the organization must develop practices and policies that encourage new faculty to feel a sense of ownership over their positions and their institution. The task for the organization is to recognize both the shared and different needs that the various generations bring with them into the workplace and then to adapt both the mentorship programming and even the larger workplace as appropriate.

PROPOSITION 5: For the theologically informed mentorship proposed in this volume to succeed, issues of diversity must not only be acknowledged but also addressed.

Mentorship that takes seriously the need to address minority communities' exclusion from and oppression by the academy and the larger society requires serious, intentional work on the part of mentors; they must address their own biases. The mentorship also needs to help mentees to confront their prejudices. According to Colón-Emeric, mentors must be able to hear stories of exclusion and pain experienced by their mentees and be willing to engage in practices of lament with their mentees. Likewise, they need to be able to hear, without countering defensively, critiques of the organization in which they have invested themselves or of their own racialized or gendered behavior. Only then can the mentoring relationship begin to address the feelings of exclusion that women and faculty of color experience in the academy. Mentors who grasp these issues, either because they personally experienced them or because they were educated in how to do so, can prove invaluable to mentees.

Although important, the aspects of mentorship described above cannot occur in isolation if women and faculty of color are to be more than guests in the academy, if genuine reconciliation is to occur, and if a new *we* is to be created. Institutions must also address their own biases and discriminatory practices. That analysis may involve organizational practices of lament and self-reflection, such as those described by Colón-Emeric in his chapter, as well as diversity work that occurs for all employees, not just mentors and mentees. Policies, procedures, and practices should be examined for explicit and implicit gendered and racial biases. Such an audit may need to be conducted by outsiders who can better see the biases than can insiders. Because these suggestions, both on the personal and on the institutional level, require the dismantling of privilege, this proposition will be the most difficult to implement. Yet the benefits, as described above in this chapter, can prove powerful for the individuals and organizations involved, as well as for the larger society and greater Christendom.

FINAL THOUGHTS

Although not without its challenges, theologically informed mentorship offers considerable promise for the future of Christian higher education. This conclusion provides several propositions, based on the work of the other contributors to this volume, by which such mentorship can be used to theologically resource faculty in their vocational callings. By providing a means through which new generations of Christian academicians can be more firmly grounded in their faith and vocations, the mission of Christian higher education can be furthered more effectively.

More important, theologically informed mentorship has the potential to equip believers for service not only to the academy but also to the world. In the words of Colón-Emeric,

> The new *we* is ecclesial; it is constituted through participation in Christ's mission by the power of the Spirit. In other words, the Christian scholar's vocation should not be self-referential but apostolic; its intellectual horizon is not the academy but the world, especially its social and existential peripheries. After Pentecost, mentoring involves the formation of habits and postures of dialogue that encounter people in their daily realities with confidence and courage. . . . The new *we* is catholic and intentionally inclusive of the voices (and dreams) of mothers and fathers from the early church and from sisters and brothers from the global church.

This certainly is a future promise!

CONTRIBUTORS

Tim Clydesdale is vice provost, dean of graduate studies, and professor of sociology at The College of New Jersey. Previously, he served on the faculty at Gordon College. He is the author of numerous articles and books, including *The Twentysomething Soul: Understanding the Religious and Secular Lives of American Young Adults* (Oxford University Press, 2019), *The Purposeful Graduate: Why Colleges Must Talk to Students About Vocation* (University of Chicago Press, 2015), and *The First Year Out: Understanding American Teens After High School* (University of Chicago Press, 2007).

Edgardo Colón-Emeric is dean of Duke University Divinity School, the Irene and William McCutchen Associate Professor of Reconciliation and Theology, and director of the Center for Reconciliation. Previously, he served as senior strategist for the Hispanic House of Studies at Duke. His work explores the intersection of Methodist and Catholic theologies and Wesleyan and Latin American experiences. He is the author of *Oscar Romero's Theological Vision: Liberation and the Transfiguration of the Poor* (University of Notre Dame Press, 2018) and *Wesley, Aquinas, and Christian Perfection: An Ecumenical Dialogue* (Baylor University Press, 2009). Colón-Emeric is an ordained elder in the North Carolina Annual Conference, directs the Central American Methodist Course of Study and the Peru Theological Initiative, and serves on the United Methodist Committee on Faith and Order and as a participant in both national and international Methodist-Catholic dialogues.

Christopher J. Devers is assistant professor of education at Johns Hopkins University and senior fellow for operations for the Lumen Research Institute. Overall, Devers is interested in applied metacognitive processes and how people learn. Specifically, he explores learning as facilitated by using videos and mobile devices in online environments. He is also interested in the scholarship of teaching and learning and student success. He has published numerous articles in publications such as *Journal of Interactive Learning Research, Journal of Educational Multimedia and Hypermedia, International Journal on E-Learning,* and *International Journal of Instructional Technology and Distance Learning.*

Margaret Diddams is the editor for *Christian Scholar's Review* and the former provost at Wheaton College. She started her academic career as an instructor and program coordinator in the Social-Organizational Psychology Department at Columbia University. Diddams then joined the faculty at Seattle Pacific University in 1993 and served as professor of industrial/organizational psychology, the director of the Center for Scholarship and Faculty Development, and assistant provost. In addition to her academic work, Diddams worked as a senior manager for Microsoft and founded The Diddams Group, a consulting practice specializing in executive coaching. She has published numerous articles in publications such as *Leadership Quarterly, Academy of Management Review, Journal of Religion and Business, Journal of College Counseling, Christian Scholar's Review, Journal of Management, Spirituality and Religion,* and *Journal of Psychology and Theology.*

Tim Elmore is the founder and CEO of Growing Leaders, an Atlanta-based nonprofit organization created to develop emerging leaders. Since founding Growing Leaders in 2003, Elmore has spoken to more than five hundred thousand students, faculty, and staff on hundreds of campuses across the country, including Stanford University, Duke University, Wake Forest University, and Ohio State University. Elmore has also provided leadership training for multiple athletic programs, including the University of Alabama, the University of North Carolina, the University of Texas, and sports teams such as the Kansas City Royals, the San Francisco Giants, the Tampa Bay Buccaneers, the Houston Rockets, and the Buffalo Bills. Elmore has written more than thirty-five books, including the best-selling *Habitudes: Images That Form Leadership Habits and Attitudes* (Growing Leaders, 2004–2019), *Artificial Maturity* (Jossey-Bass, 2001).

Generation Z Unfiltered: Facing Nine Hidden Challenges of the Most Anxious Population (Poet Gardner, 2019). His most recent book is *The Eight Paradoxes of Great Leadership* (HarperCollins, 2021). Tim has appeared on CNN's *Headline News* and *Fox & Friends* to discuss today's emerging generation, as well as in the *Washington Post*, the *Wall Street Journal*, and Forbes.com. He lives in Atlanta with his wife, Pam. (Their two adult children are both gainfully employed and have moved out of the house.)

Stacy A. Hammons is the executive director for Diversity, Equity, and Inclusion at Community Health Network (Indiana). Formerly, she was provost and professor of sociology at Indiana Wesleyan University. She has also served as an administrator and faculty member at Tabor College and Fresno Pacific University, where she taught both social work and sociology. Her research has focused on family relationships, gender, and most recently assessment and adjuncts. She has published numerous articles in publications such as the *Journal for the Scientific Study of Religion, Assessment and Evaluation in Higher Education, Journal of Continuing Higher Education,* and *American Journal of Distance Education.*

Rebecca C. Hong is senior director of educational effectiveness and assessment at Loyola Marymount University. Previously, Hong served in the roles of assistant provost for educational effectiveness, dean of curriculum and assessment, and associate professor of education at Biola University. At Biola she led a Faculty Assessment Fellows program that embraced best practices for faculty learning communities and launched the Student Assessment Scholars program that trained and elevated undergraduate and graduate students to be change-makers in their university. One of her recent publications can be found in the special issue "Assessment and Social Justice: Pushing Through Paradox" in *New Directions for Institutional Research.*

David Kinnaman is the president of the Barna Group, a leading research and communications company that works with churches, nonprofits, and businesses ranging from film studios to financial services. He is the author of the bestselling books *Good Faith: Being a Christian When Society Thinks You're Irrelevant and Extreme* (Baker Books, 2016), *You Lost Me: Why Young Christians Are Leaving Church . . . and Rethinking Faith*

(Baker Books, 2011), and *unChristian: What a New Generation Really Thinks About Christianity . . . and Why It Matters* (Baker Books, 2007). His most recent book is *Faith for Exiles: 5 Ways for a New Generation to Follow Jesus in Digital Babylon* (Baker Books, 2019). Since 1995, Kinnaman has directed interviews with nearly one million individuals and overseen hundreds of US and global research studies.

Jerry Pattengale is university professor at Indiana Wesleyan University, codirector of the Lumen Research Institute, and associate publisher for *Christian Scholar's Review*. He was one of the two founding scholars of Museum of the Bible (Washington, DC) and continues to serve as senior adviser to the museum president. Pattengale has authored dozens of books and contributes to a wide variety of publications, including the *Wall Street Journal*, *Christianity Today*, the *Washington Post*, *Inside Higher Ed*, and the *Chicago Tribune*, as well as outlets such as The History Channel, and co-authoring an award-winning TV series. The National Press Club presented him its Vivian Award in December 2021.

Todd C. Ream serves as a faculty member at Taylor University, publisher of *Christian Scholar's Review*, senior fellow for public engagement with the CCCU, and senior fellow for programming with the Lumen Research Institute. Previously, Ream served on college and university campuses in residence life, student support services, honors programs, and as a chief student affairs officer. He is the author and editor of numerous books and contributes to a wide variety of publications, including *About Campus*, *Christianity Today*, *First Things*, *Inside Higher Ed*, *Modern Theology*, *New Blackfriars*, *Notre Dame Magazine*, the *Review of Higher Education*, and *Teachers College Record*. He is presently working on a series of books concerning Theodore M. Hesburgh, CSC.

Beck A. Taylor is president of Samford University. Previously, he served as the president of Whitworth University, as dean and professor of economics for the Brock School of Business at Samford, and as associate dean for research and faculty development for the Hankamer School of Business at Baylor University, where he was also the W. H. Smith Professor of Economics. Taylor has published dozens of studies in publications such as *Review of Economics and Statistics*, *Journal of Labor Economics*, *Journal of*

Human Resources, and *Journal of Money, Credit, and Banking*. Illustrating his diverse research interests and his connections to the social sciences, Taylor has also published research concerning public health and child developmental psychology. His research has been cited in testimony given before the United States Congress, the Federal Trade Commission, and the California State Assembly, and has been referenced in publications such as the *New York Times*, the *Boston Globe*, the *Christian Science Monitor*, and *Chief Executive Magazine*.

INDEX